CULTURE SMART!

SPAIN

THE ESSENTIAL GUIDE TO CUSTOMS & CULTURE

MARIAN MEANEY AND
BELÉN AGUADO VIGUER

KUPERARD

"The real voyage of discovery consists not in seeking new landscapes, but in having new eyes."

Adapted from Marcel Proust, *Remembrance of Things Past.*

ISBN 978 1 78702 864 7

British Library Cataloguing in Publication Data
A CIP catalogue entry for this book is available
from the British Library

First published in Great Britain
by Kuperard, an imprint of Bravo Ltd
59 Hutton Grove, London N12 8DS
Tel: +44 (0) 20 8446 2440
www.culturesmart.co.uk
Inquiries: publicity@kuperard.co.uk

Design Bobby Birchall

ABOUT THE AUTHORS

MARIAN MEANEY is a teacher, translator, and interpreter who has lived and worked in Spain for more than twenty years. After graduating with honors in English and Spanish from University College, Galway, she completed a higher diploma in Education, and was awarded a scholarship to study Spanish culture at the University of Salamanca. She subsequently ran English-language academies in Malaga and Barcelona, and has advised both Spanish businesses and government organizations on international exchange programs.

BELÉN AGUADO VIGUER is a protocol, diplomacy, and tourism expert. She graduated in Tourism at the Universidad Politécnica de Valencia, gained an M.B.A. in Protocol, Event Management, and Institutional Relations at the Universidad Camilo José Cela (Madrid), and has an M.A. in International Business and Diplomacy from the University of East Anglia. After working as Coordinator of International Mobility and Development and Head of Institutional Relations at the International University of Catalonia (Barcelona), she is now CEO of Fetén (fetenparty.com), a start-up digitizing the event management service.

CONTENTS

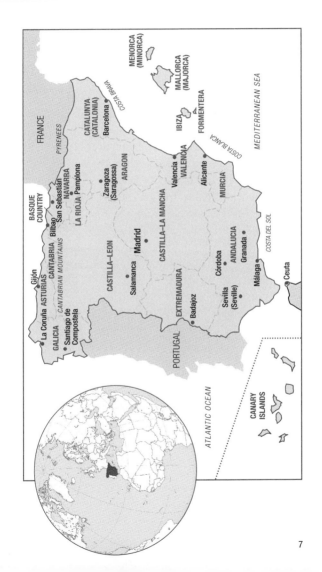

INTRODUCTION

In the popular imagination, Spain conjures up a picture of rapacious *conquistadores*, the unworldly Don Quixote, brave bullfighters, fiery flamenco dancers, and brilliant artists, from Goya and Velasquez to Picasso and Dali. All true enough—but how does the real, everyday Spain conform to these stereotypes?

The Spaniards are certainly distinctive. Visitors to Spain might be astounded by their vitality and entranced by their friendliness. Spanish people tend to be proud, passionate, spontaneous, generous, and loyal; they can also be procrastinators, individualistic to a fault, suspicious, and loud.

Spain has had a strong impact on European and world history. For almost seven hundred years under Moorish rule, Christians, Jews, and Muslims lived in harmony in Spain. Side by side, scholars from the different communities translated Greek and Roman texts, bringing the learning of classical antiquity to medieval Europe. Ironically, however, Spain did not benefit fully from the "new learning." In the wake of the Christian "reconquest" of 1492, Spain saw itself as the defender of the Catholic faith, and the Spanish Inquisition ended religious tolerance.

This, then, is the nation that enjoyed a golden age of enlightenment, that discovered America and gathered in its riches, and that left the great legacy of its culture and its language, which is today spoken by over four hundred million people, making it the second most-spoken language in the world. In the twentieth century, Spain suffered a bitter civil war and a stultifying dictatorship that lasted thirty-six years. However, it managed to emerge from the isolation of the Franco regime to become, once again, an integral part of Europe and the international arena.

Culture Smart! Spain explores the complex human realities of modern Spanish life. It describes how Spain's history and geography have created both regional differences and shared values and attitudes. It reveals what the Spaniards tend to be like at home, and in business, and how they socialize. The chapter on customs and traditions will prepare you, the visitor, for their boundless energy and inherited religious devotion. Despite being a secular state with a declining number of believers, many national celebrations are of Catholic origin. The chapters on making friends and communicating are there to help you make the very most of your visit. The better you understand the Spanish people, the more you will be enriched by your experience of this vital, warm, and varied country—where the individual is important, and the enjoyment of life is paramount.

Official Name	Reino de España (Kingdom of Spain)	Member of NATO, EU, OECD, and permanent guest of the G20
Capital City	Madrid	
Main Cities	Barcelona, Valencia, Seville, Saragossa	
Area	195,35 sq. miles (505,955 sq. km)	4,632 sq. miles (12,500 sq. km) insular (Canary and Balearic Islands)
Geography	Spain covers four-fifths of the Iberian Peninsula; it is bordered by Portugal on the western side.	Spain is divided from France by the Pyrenees on the northeastern side.
Terrain	Diversity of landscapes, including Mediterranean and Atlantic coastlines, a large central plateau, the Meseta, and several mountainous regions. Rivers mostly run east–west.	The main mountain ranges are the Pyrenees, Cantabrian Mts., Andalusian Mts., the Sierra Nevada. The main rivers are the Tagus, Ebro, and Douro.
Climate	Mainly Mediterranean	Inland, continental tendencies. In the north, temperate humid, or maritime
Population	46,700,000	
Ethnic Makeup	Four major ethnic groups, divided by language	Other ethnic minorities include *gitanos* (gypsies).
Language	Castilian (over 74%), Catalan (12%), Galician (8%), Basque (just over 1%)	

Religion	Roman Catholic 99%	
Government	Constitutional monarchy at the national level. There are nineteen regions, seventeen are autonomous communities and two autonomous cities (Ceuta and Melilla, in continental Africa).	The regions have the right to self-government under the Constitution.
Media	There are state and autonomous community television channels and private channels.	National newspapers with regional offices, include *El Pais, ABC, El Mundo, La Razón,* and *Público.*
Media (English)	Various newspapers in different cities	
Electricity	220 volts, 50 Hz	Two-prong plugs are used. Transformers are needed for US appliances.
Video/TV	Pal B system	Some systems will play NTSC TV.
Internet Domain	.es	
Telephone	Spain's country code is 34.	To dial out, dial the country code followed by a number of 9 digits. Within Spain landline numbers always start with the local prefix of 2 or 3 digits (for example, 91–Madrid, 96–Valencia).
Time	GMT + 1 hour. In summer, GMT + 2 hours	

CHAPTER ONE

LAND *&* PEOPLE

A GEOGRAPHICAL SNAPSHOT

One of the largest countries in Europe, Spain is situated on the Iberian Peninsula, which it shares with two other countries: Portugal on the west and and the Principality of Andorra to the north. The Pyrenees run across the neck of the peninsula and form Spain's border with France. The large central plateau, the Meseta, is bordered and divided by several mountain ranges. Madrid, situated at the geographical center, at an average altitude of 2,100 feet (655 m), is the highest capital city in Europe.

Although Spain has rivers that are numbered among the longest in Europe (the Tajo, Ebro, and Douro), large areas of the country such as the Levante area in the southeast and most of the Canary Islands suffer from a scarcity of water. Linked to this problem is erosion, with millions of tons of topsoil being blown away each year. However, not all of Spain is dry or barren. The deep inlets of Galicia, the Cantabrian coast,

and the snowy highlands of the Pyrenees are just a few examples of Spain's variety of landscape.

From a tourist's point of view, the coastline is immensely important. Spain has over two thousand beaches, many of them of great beauty. One out of six of the "Blue flags" given worldwide by the World Trade Organization to beaches of outstanding quality and high environmental standard is in Spain. They are grouped together under famous names corresponding to their position, such as the Costa Brava, Costa Dorada, Costa de Azahar, Costa Blanca, Mar Menor, Costa del Sol, Costa de la Luz, Rias Bajas and Rias Altas, Costa Cantábrica, Costa Canaria, and Costa Balear.

The total area of national territory is 195,350 square miles (505,955 sq. km), which includes the Canary and Balearic Islands and the two small enclaves of Ceuta and Melilla in Northern Africa. There is an incredible natural diversity to be enjoyed. As the British naturalists Chapman

The Central Massif of the Picos de Europa in Cabrales, Asturias.

and Buck commented in their book *Wild Spain* (1893): "In no other land can there be found, within a similar area, such extremes of scene and climate."

CLIMATE

Although Spain lies in the temperate zone, its mountainous nature means that there are three differing climates: generally, wet, dry, and arid.

The wet climate (Oceanic and Mountainous), with more than 30 inches (800 mm) of precipitation a year occurs along the northwestern coast of Galicia and inland to Cataluña, and includes the northeastern coastal area that borders with France. These areas show only slight variations in temperature, with mild winters and cool summers. A cloudy sky and frequent rainfall are common, although less so during the summer months.

About 72 percent of the country has a dry climate (Mediterranean and Continental), receiving between 11 and 30 inches (300–800 mm) of precipitation a year. It is characteristic of the Levante area, the coast of Cataluña and most of the Balearic archipelago; the central plateau, and the valleys of the rivers Ebro, in the northeast, and Guadalquivir in Andalucía. Summer in these areas brings a blazing sun and an intense blue sky, with occasional, short-lived, local thunderstorms.

The arid climate, defined by less than 11 inches (300 mm) of rainfall a year is found in some areas of the Levante, on the coast of Murcia (in the southeast), and in some interior areas.

The Canary Islands have a subtropical, Atlantic climate, which is generally dry except for the mountainous areas. They enjoy an almost constant temperature of just over 68°F (20°C), with only minor variations between seasons.

REGIONAL POINTS OF VIEW

Spanish people's loyalty to their country is especially evident when they travel or live abroad. Generally, they value their culture, gastronomy, climate, and the people enormously. Together, they represent what is meaningful in life for the average Spanish person. Therefore, you might be surprised to see a Spaniard passionately discussing and defending his own region against another. This is largely the result of the different perceptions the Spanish have about their history and the way it influenced their particular region.

There is, of course, no such thing as a typical Spaniard, but as in any other culture regional stereotypes abound: the entrepreneurial and greedy Catalans of the northeast, the hot-blooded and lively Andalusians of the south, and the good-natured and picaresque Castilians from the central Meseta. It is possible to distinguish people from different regions by paying attention to their accent, linguistic expressions, and their mannerisms. In the past, mountain ranges hindered communications, different climates influenced local character, and divisions arose that still have not been overcome. Long before the Catholic monarchs Ferdinand and Isabella united the kingdoms of Castile and Aragon by marriage and overthrew Muslim rule in 1492, there were various kingdoms within the peninsula, and Castilian dominance, for them, meant only a reduction in power. Spain was united in name only. The Golden Age did indeed bring great riches to the country, but not to the whole country, for most of the wealth was channeled to Castile or remained in the ports. Catalonia, which had been a major trading power, was at first not even allowed to trade with America.

The Basque Country and Catalonia fought hard for autonomy, which they finally received in 1978. Galicia, Andalucía, Asturias, and Cantabria followed, and today there are nineteen autonomous regions that make up Spain. Catalonia sees itself as more modern and cosmopolitan than the rest of the country. Some citizens and politicians often use this perception to create a distance between the Catalans and the rest of Spain, in promoting independence as a separate state.

Differences in climate, traditions, and the character of the people in some regions, highlighted by the local language and dialects, may explain an initial feeling of disorientation that a Spaniard might experience when moving to a different region.

In general, however, the modern Spaniard is proud of his country. When Franco died in 1975 he left Spain weary of dictatorship and hungry for democracy and a place in the international community. In 1986 Spain became a member of both the European Union and NATO.

A BRIEF HISTORY

It is impossible to do justice in a few pages to Spain's rich and varied history. What follows is merely a brief synopsis.

Early Inhabitants
The Iberian Peninsula has been occupied for hundreds of thousands of years. Human bones from the Middle Pleistocene (at least 280,000 years old) have been found in the Cueva Mayor ("Main Cave" at Atapuerca, Burgos) and have helped to document human evolution in Europe.

The most advanced people living on the peninsula in classical antiquity were known as the Iberians. They lived along the Mediterranean and southern Atlantic coasts, and are now thought to be natives of the peninsula. The Celts lived mainly in the north and west except for the western Pyrenees, where the Basques lived, whose origin still remains uncertain.

The Greeks came to Spain, but founded only two settlements, in the northeast. Many of the Greek artifacts unearthed in Spain were actually passed on by Phoenician middlemen. In the ninth century BCE the Phoenicians founded their first settlement at Cadiz and established themselves along the southeastern Mediterranean coast. They traded oil and wine for silver, but also brought religious ideas, skilled metalworking, and literacy to the people. This period, sometimes known as the "orientalization" of prehistoric Spain, had an important impact on Iberian culture. The number of colonies diminished toward the end of the sixth century; those remaining were closer to Carthage, the most important of the Phoenicians' western Mediterranean settlements. However, by 218 BCE the Carthaginians, under Hannibal, had pushed far up the peninsula and brought upon themselves the wrath of the Roman Empire.

The Romans
The Romans landed in Ampurias, Gerona (Catalonia), in the second century BCE to destroy the power of the Carthaginians and make Spain part of their empire. It took them two hundred years to subdue the people. They constructed roads, irrigation systems, and engineering marvels. Some impressive examples—such

Constructed between 16 and 15 BCE, the Roman theater of Mérida in
Extremadura is designated one of Spain's Twelve Treasures.

as the aqueduct at Segovia, the bridge over the Tagus
at Alcántara, or the amphitheater at Mérida—remain
to this day. Spain's current language, religion, and laws
stem from this period. Some of the upper classes in the
towns and cities of Spain formed part of the elite of
the Roman Empire. They included the philosopher
and writer Seneca, the poet Martial, and several
members of the Roman Senate, including Trajan and
Hadrian, who later became emperors.

The Visigoths arrived in the fifth century CE,
but the last Ibero-Roman strongholds did not fall
until the seventh century CE.

The Arab Influence

In the year 711, Moors from northern Africa sailed
across the mere eight miles (12.8 km) that separated

them from Spain and, within a few years, had pushed the Visigoths right back to the Cantabrian Mountains in the north of the country. They remained in Spain for over eight hundred years, a time of tolerance when Muslims, Christians, and Jews lived together in peace. Medieval Spain was the only multiracial and multireligious country in Western Europe, and much of the development of Spanish civilization in religion, literature, art, and architecture during the later Middle Ages stemmed from this fact. Many of the beautiful buildings built by the Moors—such as Seville's Giralda Tower and Alcázar and the magical Alhambra of Granada—still enchant us today.

Different emirates rose and fell during this time. One example, the Caliphate of Córdoba, produced a brilliant

Court of the Lions at the Alhambra in Granada.

civilization that lasted just over a hundred years before
splitting into a number of rival princedoms. The court
culture embraced fields as varied as historiography,
calligraphy, poetry, music, botany, medicine,
mathematics, astronomy, ivory carving, and metalwork.
The Moors stayed in Spain until 1492, although by the
second half of the thirteenth century their power had
been limited to the stronghold of Granada.

The *Reconquista*
The divisions among the Moors paralleled those
occurring in Christian Spain. The country was divided
into different kingdoms, which were unwilling to unite
forces until the second half of the fifteenth century.

Finally, Ferdinand of Aragon and Isabella of Castile
united, at least on paper, their kingdoms. In practice
during their reign each ruled his or her kingdom
independently. The saying "*Tanto monta, monta tanto,
Isabel como Fernando*" ("Both Isabella and Ferdinand
amount to the same") highlights the equal power of both
according to their prenuptial agreement, which was very
uncommon at that time. The marriage of the "Catholic
Kings" led to the *Reconquista*, or "Reconquest," the name
given to the struggle to win back the territory lost to
the "nonbelievers."

Aided by the Inquisition they set out to free Spain
from Arab domination and to achieve religious
unification. Moors and Jews, who had actively
contributed to the rise of an educated and commercial
elite, and who held many administrative posts in

Christian Spain, aroused jealousy and hatred in a population that saw itself as the defender of Christianity against the infidel.

Forcible attempts at conversion included confiscation of property, and torture, which often led to death. The Spanish Inquisition was founded in 1478 to root out heresy. After the last Moorish city, Granada, was taken in 1492, all Jews who refused to convert to Christianity were expelled. Those who converted become subject to the Inquisition, whose role was to prevent backsliding among the "New Christians."

During the Protestant Reformation, fear of heresy led the Church to oppose new ideas, making Spain retreat slowly into intellectual conservatism.

By 1609 the last of the Moors had left, and Spain was bereft of both agricultural and administrative expertise. However, some influence remained. Many Christians from other countries had also studied with the Moors. One example was the School of Translators founded in the twelfth century at Toledo, where Jewish, Christian, and Muslim scholars had worked side by side. The resulting translations into Latin brought this treasury of human knowledge and philosophy not only to Spain, but also to Italy and France, planting the seeds of the Renaissance.

The Golden Age

The conquest of Granada allowed Castile to concentrate major resources and effort on overseas exploration instead of on domestic conflicts. The support that

Christopher Columbus received from Isabella was indicative of this new policy. In 1492, during an expedition that was meant to establish a new trade route to Asia, Columbus made his great discovery of America—the New World. Spain and Portugal divided the spoils between them, and almost all of South America, Central America, North America, and the Philippines were added to the Spanish possessions.

The tomb of Christopher Columbus in Seville Cathedral.

By exploiting the indigenous population, gold and silver, the primary objective of the *conquistadores*, flowed into Spain in fabulous quantities. In the sixteenth century, Spain became the most important power in the world, with a huge empire, fleets on every sea, and a brilliant cultural, artistic, and intellectual life.

When Charles I (elected Holy Roman Emperor in 1519 as Charles V) came to the throne, Spain was still divided into separate kingdoms and principalities. However, by the time he abdicated in favor of his son, Philip II, in 1556, Spain was on its way to becoming a centralized and absolute monarchy, although Catalonia, Navarre, Aragon, Valencia, and the Basque Country were still allowed a considerable degree of autonomy. This shift of power within the country led to Catalonia, the most important trading region, not receiving any share in the new markets, and it was actually prohibited from dealing with the New World. By ridding itself of both the Jews and the Catalans, Spain deprived itself of its economically most active citizens and finally had to depend on German and Italian financiers.

Very little of the American treasure seems to have been invested in the economy. Most of it was used for display by the court, to pay for imports, for the armies abroad, and to satisfy foreign creditors. Thus Spain, with all the treasure of the New World at its command, remained a poor country.

During the sixteenth century the Church expanded its already dominant role in Spanish life, and the Spanish Inquisition reached its greatest power. At the same time the

Counter Reformation sought to reclaim Protestant Europe for the Church and to raise the spiritual tone of the Catholic countries. The Jesuit order, founded by St. Ignatius Loyola, an ex-soldier, was a major force. Its missionaries went all over the world and succeeded in converting millions to Catholicism. The life of a Jesuit was one of immense risk, and thousands of priests were persecuted or killed on their mission of conversion. However, in some countries, such as India and China, the Jesuits were welcomed as men of wisdom and science.

Education was of utmost importance to the Jesuits. In nearly every major city in Europe they established schools and colleges, and for a hundred and fifty years they were leaders in European education. (Through their loyalty to papal policies, the Jesuits were later drawn into the struggle between the papacy and the Bourbon monarchies, and in the middle of the eighteenth century they were expelled from many countries including Spain. In 1814 they were reestablished once more.)

It was also a truly "Golden Age" for Spanish arts and literature. The novel reached its highest level with Cervantes's *Don Quixote*, which has been compared to Shakespeare's *Hamlet* and Homer's *Iliad*. Written to mock the popular novels of chivalry that glorified the ideals of courtesy, constancy, bravery, and loyalty, it was also considered part of the picaresque tradition (describing the adventures of a *pícaro*, a wandering rogue). There was a profusion of great poets, such as Garcilaso de la Vega, San Juan de la Cruz, and Luis de Góngora. The theater benefited from the many

Bronze statues of Don Quixote and Sancho Panza, at the Plaza de España in Madrid.

plays of Lope de Vega, Tirso de Molina, and Calderón de la Barca. Likewise, in the world of painting Diego Velasquez, "El Greco" (Domenikos Theotokopoulos), Zurbarán, and Murillo were prominent artists of the time.

The Decline

With Spain, Philip II had also inherited Sicily, Naples, Sardinia, Milan, Franche-Comté, the Netherlands, and all the Spanish colonies. His reign is still credited with the phrase *"El imperio en el que nunca se pone el sol"* ("The empire on which the sun never sets"). However, a series of long, costly wars and revolts, capped by the defeat by the English of the "Invincible Armada" in 1588, began the steady decline of Spanish power in Europe. The nineteenth century brought invasion by Napoleon, who put his brother on the throne and started the furious conflict, referred to by the Spanish as the War of Independence and by the English as the Peninsular War (1807–14). Spain ousted France, but only with the help of the British and the Portuguese. Later came the revolt and independence of most of Spain's colonies. There were also three wars over the succession, the brief ousting of the monarchy, and the establishment of the First Republic (1873–74), when the idea of Spain as a federal state was considered. Finally, the Spanish–American War (1898) sealed its fate. Spain lost Cuba, Puerto Rico, and the Philippines to the United States, and the days of empire were over.

By the end of the nineteenth century there were deep divisions within Spanish society. The Socialist and Anarcho-Syndicalist parties began to gain a wide following among the lower classes, particularly in industrial Catalonia, rural Andalusia, and in the mining districts of Asturias. Strikes and uprisings, suppressed with great brutality, became common. The Church, which supported the landowners, aroused anticlerical feeling, which was often violent, among revolutionary, and even liberal, elements. Meanwhile, the military watched everything closely in its self-imposed role as the guardian of the core values of Spanish society.

King's Alfonso XIII's support of General Miguel Primo de Rivera's military dictatorship in 1923 led to public mistrust and an overwhelming republican majority in the elections of 1931, after Primo de Rivera's resignation in 1930. Alfonso went into exile on April 14, 1931. The government introduced a range of reforms, including autonomy for the Basque Country and Catalonia, and restrictions on the power of the Church. The conservatives feared even more changes and grouped together for the elections in 1933. Meanwhile, internal divisions among the left began to show and they ran as separate parties. They lost. The right-wing government immediately began to reverse the reforms carried out since 1931.

The Civil War

The next elections, in 1936, were won by the Popular Front, a coalition of several left-wing parties, and the reforms were reinstated. The conservatives immediately began to plan resistance. Rumors of a military coup

General Francisco Franco.

led the government to transfer several high-ranking military officers to remote postings, hoping to make communication more difficult. (Francisco Franco was sent to Morocco.) Despite their efforts, the conservative military rebellion took place on July 18. The organizers expected a quick victory. Instead, the civilian population took up arms in support of the government. The insurgents, or Nationalists, who soon came under the leadership of General Francisco Franco, embraced most conservative groups, notably the monarchists, most of the army officers, the clericalists, the landowners and industrialists, and the Carlists (a right-wing political movement, opposed to liberal secularism and economic and political modernism).

The right-wing rebels realized they would now have to look for outside help, and appealed to the fascist dictatorships in Italy, Germany, and Portugal, who sent supplies and men. The navy remained loyal to

"El Generalísimo," Spanish Civil War poster of the socialist trade-union UGT, showing a caricature of a foreign-supported Franco followed by a general, a capitalist, and a priest, 1937.

the government, so Hitler's pilots began transporting soldiers and equipment from Spanish Morocco. Their destruction the following April of the Basque city of Guernica shocked the world.

Despite almost universal support for the Republic among British intellectuals and widespread support among the working classes, the British conservative government preferred not to act. Not only did it fear a larger international fight, but it was also more in sympathy with the rebels' conservative policies than the government's. France sympathized with the government but, fearing its own army, felt in too weak a position to do more. After sending a score of planes they proposed a nonintervention policy that was maintained throughout the war (although Germany and Italy merely ignored it). The left-wing Loyalists received some meager support only from Russia and Mexico.

The 1936 Spanish election had already been considered a great victory for the working classes, so the military uprising was seen as an assault against working people's interests everywhere. The rapid intervention of foreign troops made the Civil War international and it became an example of the growing worldwide struggle between fascism and democracy. Foreign volunteers arrived to fight on both sides. Those who fought with the Loyalists were called the International Brigades. They came from a variety of left-wing groups but were nearly always led by Communists. This created problems with other Republican groups, such as the Workers' Party of Marxist Unification (POUM) and the Anarchists, who provoked several days of rioting and fighting in May 1937 in Barcelona. This internal dissension on the Left damaged their spirit and weakened their army.

Despite military inferiority and bloody internal divisions, the Loyalists made a remarkably determined stand, particularly in central Spain. By the beginning of 1938, however, the territory held by the Loyalists had shrunk drastically, and with the fall of Barcelona in January 1939 the war was almost over. Madrid surrendered in March and the Loyalist government and many thousands of refugees fled into France.

In total, about 3.3 percent of the Spanish population died during the war, with another 7.5 percent being injured. Available information suggests that there were between 500,000 and 600,000 deaths from all causes during the Spanish Civil War, of which 220,000 were a direct result of the Francoist repression. The economic blockade of Republican-controlled areas caused malnutrition in the civilian population that is believed to have resulted in the deaths of around 25,000 people. After the war it is claimed that Franco's government arranged for the execution of 100,000 Republican prisoners, and it is estimated that another 35,000 later died in concentration camps.

Franco's Dictatorship
A dictatorship was set up under Franco that restored the favored position of the Church and returned its

confiscated properties. The Movimiento Nacional (National Movement) became the only political party, encompassing all right-wing groups, and the leftist opposition was suppressed. The Cortes (Parliament) and Catalan and Basque autonomy were abolished— although the Cortes was reestablished in 1942. Although it gave aid to the Axis (Germany and Italy) during the Second World War, Spain did not actually take part in the fighting. However, the United Nations, refusing to recognize the constitutionality of the Franco regime, in 1946 urged its members to break diplomatic relations with Spain; this resolution was not rescinded until 1950. An agreement with the United States in 1953 provided for US bases in Spain and for economic and military aid. Spain entered the United Nations in 1955.

Growing political unrest, partly over the problem of succession to the Franco regime, became increasingly evident in the 1950s, and at the start of the 1960s the Church, which had long been silent, began to voice some opposition to aspects of the repressive dictatorship. In 1962 a series of strikes, beginning in the coalfields of Asturias, indicated widespread discontent. Student demonstrations also occurred.

Basque separatism posed another serious problem for the regime. Their terrorist organization, ETA (Euskadi ta Askatasuna), fought against the regime. Its greatest success was the murder of Franco's prime minister, Carrero Blanco, in 1973. During this period ETA enjoyed a lot of public support, but this changed once democracy had been restored.

A new organic law (constitution) was announced by Franco in 1966. It separated the post of head of government from chief of state, provided for direct election of about one-quarter of the members of the Cortes, gave married women the vote, made religious freedom a legal right, and ended government control of the labor unions. The forming of new political parties was still discouraged. Press censorship was ended in 1966, but strong guidelines remained.

Economically, Spain progressed dramatically in the 1960s and early 1970s, stimulated in part by the liberal economic policies espoused by Opus Dei (a Roman Catholic lay order promoting Christian values, which worked to suppress liberalism and immorality—controversial among Catholics because of its secretive nature, emphasis on discipline, and its conservatism and wealth). Growth was particularly pronounced in the tourist, automobile, and construction industries.

The Transition

In 1969 Franco named his successor, Juan Carlos, the son of the legitimate heir to the throne, the king-in-exile Alfonso XIII. Juan Carlos had sworn an oath of allegiance to Franco and his regime and seemed to be willing to maintain it. In fact, he held reformist aspirations. The death of Franco on November 20, 1975, and the accession of Juan Carlos as king two days later, opened a new era: the peaceful transition to democracy.

Arias Navarro, the conservative head of the government, was incapable of making the democratic transition that the king supported. When he resigned in 1976, Adolfo Suárez Gonzalez, a former Francoist minister, replaced him. Suárez entered office promising that elections would be held within one year, and his government moved to enact a series of laws to liberalize the new regime.

Spain's first elections since 1936 were held on June 15, 1977. Suárez and his new party, Unión de Centro Democrático (UCD), were returned with 34 percent of the vote. Under Suárez, the new Parliament set about drafting a democratic constitution that was overwhelmingly approved by voters in a national referendum in December 1978. Varying levels of autonomy were granted to the Basque Country, Catalonia, and the other regions in Spain.

However, this was not enough for some of the Basque separatists. ETA continued to commit murders, although the violence has abated since the 1990s when many leaders were arrested. Confronted by terrorism and economic recession, the UCD disintegrated into factions and, after heavy defeats in local elections, Suárez resigned in January 1981.

The inauguration of Leopoldo Calvo Sotelo, also a member of the UCD, was interrupted by an attempted military coup led by Lieutenant Colonel Antonio Tejero, who occupied the Cortes on February 23, 1981, and held the government and the deputies for eighteen hours. The coup failed, thanks to King Juan Carlos' resolute support of the democratic constitution. This was a turning point as the population accepted the king as a true champion of democracy, not a pawn of the old regime. Calvo Sotelo was left with the task of restoring confidence in democracy. His most notable achievement was Spain's entry into NATO in 1982.

The election of October 1982 marked the final break with the Francoist legacy by returning the Partido Socialista Obrero Español (PSOE) under its leader, Felipe González, with a solid majority to the Cortes. This was the first government in which none of the Partido Socialista

Felipe González leader of the Partido Socialista Obrero Español (PSOE), who won the country's election in 1982.

Obrero Español members had served under Francoism, and it paved the way toward a new future. Spain became a member of the European Community in 1986, and in 1992 the country achieved prominence with the Expo '92 World's Fair in Seville and the Olympic Games in Barcelona. PSOE remained in power until 1996, when a center-right government took office. José María Aznar López, leader of the Partido Popular (PP) became prime minister in coalition with the Catalan nationalists. Aznar introduced a government austerity and privatization program, and the economy experienced significant economic growth. In 1999 Spain became part of the European Union's single currency plan and, benefiting from the prosperous economy, Aznar led the PP to a parliamentary majority in the March 2000 elections. Spain finally became a stable democracy.

THE POLITICAL LANDSCAPE TODAY

However, much has happened since that moment. After more than thirty years of power alternating between the two main political parties, the center-left PSOE and center-right to right-wing PP, a new scenario emerged in the spring of 2011 alongside the popular movement of the Spanish Revolution, which saw thousands of people camped out in the main squares of the country's major cities calling for a "real democracy" in which the people would be better represented. The movement acted as a catalyst for political change, leading to the entry of new players into the political arena. Three national parties emerged and gained significant support—Podemos (We can), a more left-wing party; Ciudadanos (Citizens), a center to center-right party positioning itself as the only real alternative to the recent decline of PP (who had their worst results ever in the 2019 elections); and Vox, which echoes the recent rise of the far right in the rest of Europe. The most immediate consequence of this new political reality is the fragmentation of power, which has changed Spain from a two party to a multiparty system. Thus, for the first time in the modern history of Spain, the political parties are being obliged to set aside their differences and find a way to govern together.

THE REGIONS

"The Iberians never would amalgamate, never would … put their shields together—never would sacrifice their own local private interest for the general good," said the nineteenth-century English traveler and writer Richard Ford. The Spaniards are generally very proud of their own regions, which is why they can sometimes seem individualistic. This pride in their traditions, customs, and language underlies the need for self-government, leading to the creation of the Comunidades Autónomas (Autonomous Communities). Today, Spain is divided into nineteen regions: two of them, Ceuta and Melilla in North Africa, are "autonomous cities," and the other seventeen "autonomous communities" are the Basque

Country, Catalonia, Galicia, Andalusia, Asturias, Aragon, Balearic Islands, Canary Islands, Cantabria, Castile-León, Castile-La Mancha, Extremadura, Madrid, Murcia, Navarre, La Rioja, and Valencia.

For the first five years the central government allowed all regions control of the organization of institutions, urban planning, public works, housing, environmental protection, cultural affairs, sports and leisure, tourism, health and social welfare, and the cultivation of the regional language, where there was one. After five years they could accede to "full autonomy," but the meaning of this phrase was not clearly defined.

The transfer of powers to the autonomous governments has been determined in an ongoing process of negotiation between the individual communities and the central government. This process has given rise to repeated disputes. The communities, especially Catalonia, have complained that the central government has dragged its feet in ceding powers and in clarifying financial arrangements. Not all regions have the same powers. For instance, the Basque Country and Catalonia have their own police forces, and Navarra has a different financial arrangement from the others. Indeed, some regions deserve a special mention.

Due to their distinctive cultures and history, the Spanish Constitution from 1978 granted the regions of Catalonia, Galicia, and the Basque Country the maximum level of autonomy. This is why they are known as "the historic nations." Situated in the north of the country, near France, they were under Moorish rule for a very brief period, if at all. Just like the other seventeen regions, they have their own traditions and customs, however they also maintain their own languages (not dialects) —Catalan, Euskera, and Galician. With Spanish, these three are considered official languages within their respective regions.

Galicia is the poorest of the regions, and is not as vocal about autonomy as the others. The Basque Country and Catalonia are the most industrialized areas in Spain, and have a different work ethic from the rest of the country. A significant number of their citizens do not appreciate being referred to as Spanish, and show fierce loyalty to their own flags—the *ikurriña* in the Basque Country and the *senyera* in Catalonia—which today can be seen hanging from some balconies and windows in support of independence and have become a matter of political debate. Andalusia is the largest region in Spain, visited by many thousands of tourists each year. Despite being very distinctive from the other regions, for many it epitomizes traditional rural Spain.

The Basque Country (Euskal Herria)

The Basques occupied the northern part of Spain (and part of France) thousands of years before the rise of the Roman Empire. Their region is known as Euskal Herria, or Euskadi in their own language, *Euskera*. This language is neither Latin-based nor related to any of the Indo-European languages, and there is much speculation about its roots. Researchers have linked it to languages in many other parts of the world, but none of these links can be proven.

Basque people can seem very different from their neighbors. Physically they tend to be taller and sturdier, and they have the highest proportion of rhesus-negative blood in Europe (25 percent), and one of the highest percentages of type O blood (55 percent). Fiercely independent, they retained their own sovereignty until nearly the fourteenth century. Even then they were only nominally integrated and could veto laws by saying "we obey but do not comply." It was not until the nineteenth century that the centralist government in Madrid deprived them of these rights. Fearing for their language and their culture, they began pressing for reforms and for greater autonomy. However, the Civil War and fascist dictatorship that followed prohibited all outward signs of Basque identity, and the very speaking of *Euskera* was declared illegal.

The Basques suffered terribly during the Spanish Civil War and under the subsequent oppression, which explains why some separatists gradually began to organize themselves clandestinely. The terrorist group Euskadi Ta Askatasuna (ETA), in *Euskera* "Basque Country and Freedom," was created in 1959 with the aim of fighting for their independence. Since then, the organization has committed more than 700 attacks, killed around 900 people, and kidnapped approximately 90 people. Although many of their members left once autonomy was achieved, they have continued terrorist attacks throughout Spain, hoping to achieve complete independence for the Basque Country. However, they no longer command the support of the majority.

Despite its strong industrial character, owing to its mining sector, the Basque region has a green and rugged landscape, wild coastlines, and Michelin-starred restaurants. A famous local snack is the *pintxo*, small slices of bread with different toppings, fastened with a toothpick. Many of the renowned Spanish chefs are, in fact, Basque. People drink more here, however; drunkenness is not as frowned upon as in other areas of the country. Spanish is the dominant language, which is just as well, as you will not understand a word of Euskera. The Basques are a proud people, with a rich heritage that merits respect.

Catalonia (Catalunya)

Catalonia is situated on the northwestern Mediterranean coast, bordering France and Andorra. Its population exceeds seven million people, with 75 percent living in or near the capital, Barcelona. Commercially successful, it is the richest region of Spain and considers itself more "European" than other areas. The local language, Catalan, stems from Latin but sounds different from Spanish, especially because of its accent and rhythm. Many two-syllable Latin words are reduced to one. For example, *noctem* (night) becomes *noche* in Spanish and *nit* in Catalan, and *totus* (all) is *todo* in Spanish and *tot* in Catalan.

Like the Basques, many Catalans have never felt part of Spain. Despite being subject to Castile and

Aragon since 1479, Catalonia maintained its own local government until the eighteenth century and the Spanish War of Succession (1701–14). It was never fully independent as we understand the term today, but part of the larger competing Spanish monarchies whose territories extended beyond the Catalan province. Today, Catalan is still spoken in Alguers and in Sardinia.

On September 11, 1714, the Spanish Bourbon troops entered Barcelona. It was like 1066 for the English. The government was suppressed, Spanish became the language of administration, universities were closed, and Catalonia came totally under the control of Madrid. During Franco's dictatorship, under the motto "One nation, one language, one sword," Catalan, like other regional languages and dialects, was not permitted in schools nor visible in the cities. It was regarded as a sign of nationalism and was only gradually allowed in public toward the end of the regime. Nowadays, the Catalan region is mostly bilingual and, with the exception of some rural areas, both languages are used daily and the old institutions have been reestablished.

When autonomy was granted, the reforms started. Catalonia became one of the regions with the highest level of autonomy in comparison with other European regions. Its government manages a network of Catalan delegations abroad. An undercurrent of independentism has always remained and flared up over the past decades. The region has been governed by a nationalist right-wing party for the past forty years. In 2017 the Catalan independence movement became stronger and louder. Some events that summarize that turbulent period are, for example, an illegal referendum, a unilateral declaration of independence, the exile of the Catalan president to Belgium, and the imposition of the 155 Rule by the central government, by which the community remained under its direct control during four tense months. Referred to as "the Catalan conflict" or "the Catalan matter," it became a daily topic in all Spanish and many international media outlets. The matter is still unresolved today and has led to what many consider a major and most unfortunate consequence: the social fragmentation of the Catalan population, which today is deeply divided with around 50 percent supporting each side. Even within families and among friends the issue is often avoided or a reason for disagreement.

As a consequence of the scarcity of work in some regions of Spain, a large number of immigrants had moved to Catalonia during the Franco regime, attracted by the industrial activity allocated to the community at that time. As the numbers grew (a million in the 1960s alone), Spanish language and customs began to take over. It was a culture shock for both sides. The Catalans expected their regional traditions to be accepted and adopted, while the newcomers, could not see why they should be expected to change. After all, they were still in their own country.

The Catalan people have few of the traits considered to be characteristically Spanish. They are hardworking,

entrepreneurial, reliable, and serious. Other Spaniards
think of them as despotic, greedy, and materialistic.
They might not be as spendthrift, or generous, as the
others (the term depending on your point of view).
You will not often see them buying rounds of drinks,
but they will pay for their own. They might not seem
as friendly as their compatriots, nor might they meet
up for a drink after work, but this is due to a natural
reserve on their part. They are polite and generally,
if asked, will help you, but they will not intrude.
Catalonia is probably the most international region
of Spain and many different languages can be heard
spoken in the streets. Life is a bit more northern
European, but you may miss the warm welcome of
other parts of Spain.

Galicia

Galicia is the other region of Spain that has its own
language and nationalistic feeling. It is situated in the
cold, wet, northwest corner of the peninsula. It shares
a similar climate and mastery of poetry, songs, and
music with the Celtic countries (Ireland, Wales, and
Scotland). Despite the emphasis on its Celtic links,
there is no evidence that this region had any more
contact with the Celts than any other.

Unlike the Basque and Catalan regions, Galicia
remains relatively poor, agricultural, and dominated
by rural society. It is estimated that for the last five
centuries one in three Galician males has had to
leave his homeland to work in another part of Spain,

Europe, or South America. In some parts of South America the word *gallego* (meaning "Galician") is a synonym for "Spaniard." (One of the most famous descendants of Galician immigrants is Fidel Castro.)

Galician nationalism, which appeared as early as the 1840s, recalled a mythical Golden Age when the medieval kingdom of Galicia existed. There had indeed been a king of Galicia who was crowned in 1111; the kingdom was partitioned some years later, however, and the southern part would become Portugal. The northern part fell into disorder until it was incorporated into the kingdom of Castile in 1483.

Despite a study in 1990 finding that 63 percent of the population of Galicia speak and understand *galego* (the Galician spelling of the word for their language), it is not used by the middle and upper classes and is therefore not linked to social progression. Many families now bring up their children to speak Spanish.

Franco was originally from Galicia, but the region did not profit from the dictatorship. Forgotten or ignored by most governments, as they wield no power, the Galicians are generally mistrustful, hardworking, and hospitable. Among other Spaniards they have a reputation for caution and guile. However, their region is a joy to visit in the summer, when festivals abound in the villages. The cooler climate and beautiful views complement the fresh seafood and a wide variety of regional white wines. This is also the preferred season to set out on the Santiago pilgrimage route (El Camino de Santiago). The pilgrimage departs from several points in Spain and meets in the Galician capital, Santiago de Compostela. The lack of modernization does not generally bother tourists, but, on the contrary, seems to add to the attraction to the point of making them feel the *morriña,* a Galician expression meaning nostalgia or longing.

Andalusia

Andalusia covers approximately 33,694 square miles (87,268 sq. km), or 17.3 percent of Spanish territory. This makes it the largest single region, with an area greater than countries such as Belgium or the Netherlands. It is probably one of the best-known regions of Spain, as it embraces the Costa del Sol and its enviable climate. However, the interior can be harsh in winter and exhausting in summer, when temperatures can reach 113°F (45°C). Estepa, near Seville, is known as *la sartén* (the frying pan) because of the heat.

Traditionally, much of Andalusia consisted of vast estates with absentee landlords and casual laborers. Poverty led to migration, especially from the 1950s to the 1970s, and to subsidies by the central government after the dictatorship. From 1982 and for more than ten years "*las malas lenguas*" (spiteful tongues) said that the President of Spain, Felipe González, who was from Seville, favored his own region. For instance, expressways in the Basque Country and Catalonia are toll operated, while those in Andalusia are mostly free.

The 1992 Expo World Fair in Seville, which celebrated Spain's role in the discovery of America, was as important to Andalusia as the Olympics were to Catalonia. The infrastructure was improved and a large part of Seville was modernized. The region now has more than 15,000 miles (24,000 km) of expressways and highways, and some of the best international airports in the world. The rail links have also improved beyond any expectation, and it is now possible to travel from Seville to Madrid in just two and a half hours taking the high-speed train AVE.

Despite all the modernization, it is still possible to step into a village and sample a taste of the "real" Spain. Nothing can compare with the white villages of Andalusia, sparkling beneath the clear blue skies. Even along the Costa del Sol, the villages of Casares, Manilva, and Mijas are easily accessible.

Andalusia is the heart of some of the most famous Spanish folklore. Here you can find the true magic of flamenco and see bullfighting at its most authentic. *Don Juan*, *Carmen*, and other well known tales are set here. The list of Andalusian festivals is endless, and the openness of the people makes it a very appealing place to visit and join in.

Unlike the inhabitants of the other regions mentioned above, the Andalusians do generally have some of the characteristics considered to be typically Spanish. They are a friendly, hospitable, generous, and spontaneous people, who find few obstacles to making the most of their day. If you are only spending a short time in Spain, visiting Andalusia might be your best choice.

MAJOR CITIES

Madrid and Barcelona

Madrid, with a population of 3.3 million, and Barcelona, with 1.63 million, are the two largest cities in Spain. Madrid has been the capital since the reign of Philip II in the mid-sixteenth century. Its position in the geographical center of the country is symbolic. "La Puerta del Sol" (Gate of the Sun) in the heart of the city is known as the "*kilómetro cero*" of Spain (the zero

kilometer of the Spanish radial motorways). Despite the autonomy of the regions, centralization continues. It may seem a bourgeois, grand, and rather suffocating sort of city on first acquaintance; however, it is open to all—its temperament having been formed by the influx of citizens from a diverse country, a large empire, and the accompanying army of bureaucrats.

Barcelona is the largest city on the Mediterranean, and its reputation as a trading center is two thousand years old. For many years it was the economic hub of

The Royal Palace of Madrid, the official residence of the royal family. Although only used for ceremonial purposes, it is the largest functioning royal palace in Europe.

the country, while Madrid was the center of government and administration. Now they compete for the international market.

The 1992 Olympic Games were supremely important for Barcelona, enabling it to prove its professionalism on the international stage. It was also a chance to rehabilitate the old city. A belt of decrepit factories was removed, and the seashore was extended and opened. The roads were improved to make better communications between the city and the rest of the region. The Games were a huge success.

The rivalry between Spain's two preeminent cities is notorious, and nowhere is it more evident than in football. Real Madrid and Barcelona have their fans not only in Spain but throughout Europe. Since the 1940s their matches, referred to as "*el clásico*" (the classic), overshadow any others played in the country. During Franco's rule a win for Barcelona was seen by the Catalans as a victory against the dictator. Today it is a question of being the best.

Despite the fact that Madrid is the seat of government and home of the royal family, almost all the ideas that have shaped Spain's modern history—republicanism, federalism, anarchism, syndicalism, and communism— have found their way into Spain by way of Catalonia. In his book *The New Spaniards*, John Hooper adds that fashions, whether in clothing, philosophy, or art, are usually accepted in Barcelona years before Madrid.

Both cities have a wealth of things for the visitor to do. A visit to Madrid must include the great monuments to history and culture: the Royal Palace; the Prado

Museum with its extensive collection of works by Goya, Velázquez, and El Greco; the Reina Sofía Modern Art Museum, home of Picasso's *Guernica*; and the Thyssen-Bornemísza Museum, which traces the history of art from thirteenth-century Italy to modernism. When night falls, Madrid bustles. The bars are full, and overflow on to the sidewalks on summer evenings. When on holiday, recharge your batteries at *siesta* time, and prepare to join in the fun.

In Barcelona, take the time to amble through the narrow lanes of the Gothic Quarter, where you will find the imposing cathedral whose construction began in the thirteenth century and continued for the next six hundred years. A stroll down La Rambla takes you past the Liceu opera house, recently renovated after being burned down in 1994. This promenade is always bustling with shoppers, and street entertainers perform along its length. At its end, the great statue of Christopher Columbus looks out to sea and the new marina stretches before you.

See the Picasso and Miró Museums, and Gaudi's soaring, unfinished cathedral, the Sagrada Familia, which is expected to be completed by 2026 and surprisingly only obtained its building license in 2019. Then relax at a street café (*cafetería*) among the amazing buildings, and do a little "people-watching." A busy, cosmopolitan city, where ancient and modern stand side by side, Barcelona will never disappoint you.

VALUES & ATTITUDES

For many years Spain has been one of the world's main tourist destinations. In 2019, before the coronavirus pandemic, it was the second most visited country in the world. Spain's Mediterranean climate, famous culture, folklore, and gastronomic tradition all contribute to the festive and relaxed atmosphere tourists enjoy when visiting the country. The summer heat makes it difficult to work, and the balmy evenings are perfect for outdoor socializing rather than staying inside. As in most countries, the further south you go, the more relaxed the people become. The Spanish character, generally cheerful, friendly, and hospitable, has reinforced their image as intense hedonists.

Perhaps these traits stem from fatalism, for they have little or no faith in institutions, or in established authority, and do not believe they can change things. For centuries the Spanish were militant Catholics, defenders of a faith preaching that suffering in this life brings rewards in the next. Suffering is therefore accepted as a part of life, so when the opportunity arises for pleasure they dive in.

An element of risk appeals to them—and they admire the man who faces death in the bullring. The Jesuits, their great teaching order, went where there was the most danger. Heretics were burned at the stake. Their commitment was all or nothing.

Spain lies on the edge of Europe, and has been cut off from it during different periods. Moorish culture left its mark upon the country—especially in the south, where the Moors remained unconquered for over seven hundred years—and it was said that Africa began south of the Pyrenees. The famous Spanish pride, sense of honor, and *machismo* come from this period. Fighting between various aspirants to the throne kept the Spanish occupied for many years, and the Church's fear of "heresy" held new ideas at bay. Even in the twentieth century, Franco closed the doors to the outside world for much of his dictatorship. This eventually kept the country free from involvement in the Second World War. Social values were conservative, promoting social order and traditional Catholic values—bearing hardship in this life in the expectation of a reward in the next, respect for authority, and acceptance of Church teaching on moral questions. The latter has become less common, especially among young people, who are generally more sceptical about religion and the Catholic Church.

During the sixties hundreds of thousands of people had to leave rural areas to find work in the cities, and many others emigrated to France, Germany, and Switzerland in search of better opportunities. Away from their roots, their ideas began to change. Then tourists started to arrive in increasing numbers, bringing, along with their money, both the materialism and the democratic values of northern Europe. Similar movements are happening today. In 2014 more than a million young students emigrated in an attempt to escape the economic crisis. Still Spain takes its place among the foremost nations of the world and its process of change and development is ongoing.

THE FAMILY

In Spain the family is all-important, and family ties are very strong. The elderly are respected, and in some cases three generations still live together. This is changing as families get smaller or have to leave their hometowns, but in general family members still live near each other and maintain contact. An extended family of twenty

Strong family ties remain a key value.

or thirty people will often gather together to celebrate anniversaries, *santos* (see page 90), and other special occasions. Weddings tend to be the largest and most important family event for Spanish people.

Spanish pride is not limited to Spanish culture. It also involves personal success and they happily brag about themselves when they believe they have a reason to do so. Spaniards usually keep their private lives to themselves, and manage their problems within the family. The financial crisis and the need for support has brought people closer together.

During the Franco regime, Spanish law discriminated strongly against married women. They needed their husbands' approval, known as the *permiso marital*, for almost all economic activities, including employment, ownership of property, or even travel away from home. Significant reforms of this system were begun shortly before Franco's death, and have continued since then. For centuries the Catholic moral code had set stringent standards of sexual conduct for women (but not for men); restricted their career opportunities, but honored their role as wives and, most important, mothers; and prohibited divorce, contraception, and abortion, but permitted prostitution.

After the return of democracy in 1975, the change in the status of women was dramatic. The *permiso marital* was abolished, and the sale of contraceptives and divorce were legalized in 1978 and 1981. In that last year the parts of the civil code that dealt with family finances were also reformed. Abortion, until 2010 only allowed in special cases such as rape, malformed fetus, or if it posed a risk to the mother's life, became legal when the "Ley Orgánica 2/2010" entered into force in July of that year. In 2014 the government adopted some modifications after failing in its attempt to abolish it.

By 1984, 33 percent of adult women had entered the workforce and approximately 46 percent of Spain's university enrollment was female. Also, in recent years there has been increased engagement with and awareness by women of all ages of the salary gap, gender violence, and other related issues. Yet despite this seemingly painless emancipation working women are often still expected to run the house and take care of the children. Since 1970 the size of the average family has decreased from 3.8 persons to 1.36, the lowest in the world after Italy (2.1 is considered necessary for the regeneration of the population), and few children are born outside marriage. Spain now has the lowest marriage rate in the European Union. Many lay the blame for this on a more materialistic society, but it is also a result of women having to balance their workload with their duties at home. Usually the younger generations are not expected to contribute financially to the family economy, but to save for their own future, although this has changed significantly since the beginning of the economic crisis in 2008.

In one regard, however, Spanish women have always been liberated: their name. All Spaniards have two surnames (from both father and mother), so when Pilar Pujol Fernández marries Jaime Iglesias González, she will not, officially, change her name—although she may be known as *la señora de González*. On legal documents she will sign her maiden name. Their son, Pepe, will take the first surnames of his father and of his mother, and will be known as Pepe Iglesias Pujol.

Children are an integral part of society and a source of joy. Discipline is important, but in recent years issues related to the so-called "culture of effort" have been hotly debated among parents and educators. Of all European students the Spanish dedicate the most hours to homework, yet it has been estimated that their effort does not translate into high academic results when compared with the results of other European countries.

In the past, tertiary students used to have to study at local universities, whereas today they are more open to traveling abroad and attending foreign institutions. Spain sends and receives the most Erasmus students.

The old values are being questioned: girls have more options when they leave school, fewer people are getting married, and divorce is now available. People have accepted the need for residential homes to care for the sick and the elderly, but still find it difficult to accept help from outside the family. The role of the Spanish family will continue to adapt to circumstances.

FRIENDS AND ACQUAINTANCES

Spain is known as one of the friendliest places to visit in Europe. You will be welcomed everywhere, and invited to join in. However, your new Spanish friends probably extend this welcome to all newcomers, and this will not necessarily lead to a deep friendship. The Spaniards have many acquaintances, or as they say "friends to hang out with," but not always so many good friends. Accept that, and enjoy yourself.

The Spanish love talking, and will never miss a chance for conversation. Their enthusiasm can be loud and emotional. They are usually expressive, also when it comes to physical touch. Other than their family, close friends mean a great deal to Spaniards. If you do become really friendly with them you will e considered one of the family. "*Mi casa es tu casa*" ("My house is your house") means just that.

You Mustn't Be Alone!

Sara went to her friend's wedding in a small town near Seville. The wedding was at the beginning of Semana Santa (Holy Week), a time of great celebrations in that region. During the meal she was asked where she would be spending the holiday. When she said she would be going back to her apartment alone they were aghast, and she ended up spending the week at the home of one of the guests she had only just met. She was taken to all the local events, and even became an honorary member of one of the local "brotherhoods."

PRIDE, HONOR, AND *MACHISMO*

The Spaniards are proud of their region, and of their lifestyle in general, but they are also very critical and will quickly point out the negative side of things. Do *not* join in. If there is something that can offend Spanish people, it is being critical of a matter of national concern. Especially if they consider you not to be sufficiently well informed. They are not inviting comments from you, and any negative attitude on your part could be taken personally. Ironically, the pride and self-confidence Spaniards transmit does not often correspond to the image they have of themselves. Although any self doubt is quickly forgotten when La Roja (the national football team known as "the ed one") wins a match.

Family pride and honor have always been very important, and an unfaithful wife or pregnant unmarried daughter would lead to shame for the whole family. The word *macho* means male (of any species), and *machismo* describes a certain type of behavior, especially toward women. Under the previous regime the man was the breadwinner and the one who *llevaba los pantalones* (wore the trousers). However, as women's role in society is changing, so too are men's attitudes. Women's opinions in politics and society are equally respected. Nevertheless, many women still suffer from professional inequality and receive lower salaries than their male counterparts.

BEATING THE SYSTEM

In the seventeenth century the "picaresque" novel appeared. It described an anti-hero, or rogue (*el pícaro*), trying to beat the system in a harsh world in any way he could. All Spaniards can identify with him. The difference between rich and poor has been maintained by those who govern, so the Spanish look upon the government and the civil service as the enemy. Nearly forty years under a dictatorship probably did not help. Taxes are levied for the benefit not of the country, but of the government, and are assumed to be lining someone's pocket. There are many proverbs in Spanish that convey this idea, such as "*Quien hizo la ley, hizo la trampa.*" ("Whoever made the law made the loophole.") There have been countless cases against corrupt politicians who have misused their public position. It is almost expected. So the citizen bends rules and tries his or her luck. Being found out is the only crime here.

The Spanish civil service follows an old-fashioned and slow system. Offices are usually open to the public in the mornings only (as are most banks, although this has started to change), and not always daily. Despite long lines the staff (*funcionarios*) do not easily forgo their breakfast or *almuerzo* (a snack between 10:00 a.m. and 12 noon). You may be sent from one office to another, told to bring four photocopies today, and five tomorrow. However, Spain has become more efficient since its entry into the European Community.

Studying the Paperwork

Two students arrived in Madrid one weekend, having won a scholarship to study in Spain. They had been told to go to a particular office to arrange to receive their scholarship money. They went there on the Monday morning, to be told after a long wait that they would have to collect various documents from a different office. The other office opened only on Monday and Wednesday mornings. It was closed by the time they got there, so they had to stay two extra days in Madrid—just to get a few papers stamped.

The *Gestor Administrativo*

If you have to deal with officialdom, always take plenty of photocopies, photo ID, and a long book so that you have something to do while waiting in the interminable lines. You will be better treated if you can speak the language, or have a translator. Best of all, leave it in the hands of a *gestor administrativo* (the administration manager). This is a person who has been trained to advise you on the necessary papers for any transactions with the government. His job is to deal with all this time-consuming paperwork. For instance, to get a driver's license renewed involves going to several offices, waiting in each, and losing a whole morning, at least. Most people will give the necessary documentation to their *gestor*, who will do it for them for a fee.

EGOTISM

The Spanish have very little civic or public spirit, as you can judge from the litter they throw around. They generally take very personally the duty of furthering their interests, or those of their own families and closest circle, and benefiting their local community is unlikely to be a priority.

Many are often suspicious of people, expecting an ulterior motive of personal gain. Ian Gibson, who has lived in Spain since 1978, also adds in his book *Fire in the Blood*, "Protest of any kind was futile as well as dangerous in Franco's Spain, and the result is that Spaniards today are still not as energetic as they should be in standing up against petty officialdom." They became fatalistic, and did not bother to question things. The individual does not generally put himself out for the common good.

However, the public conscience is being awakened. Some examples of this change are evident in the widespread sense of solidarity with those suffering as a result of the financial crisis. There are massive marches supporting the victims of terrorist attacks, and the high rate of organ donations has positioned Spain as the world leader in this area.

TOLERANCE AND PREJUDICE

The Spaniards consider themselves tolerant. Friends will voice totally different political opinions, and this leads to heated arguments but does not affect their friendship. After Franco's death the transition to political pluralism came about with very little violence or vengeance. The Spaniards seem to have buried the past for the good of the present and future, but perhaps this is because the wounds are still raw. (Recently there have been more appeals to investigate particular cases from the Civil War and dictatorship.)

Once state censorship of magazines and films was relaxed in 1976 and in 1978, the market for pornography flourished. In a country where *Playboy* had been outlawed until 1976, this and other foreign "adult" magazines were soon considered tame, and were outsold by Spanish publications. Throughout Spain's large cities, uncensored sex films are readily available in government-licensed "X" cinemas, and prostitutes and brothels freely advertise their services in even the most serious press.

On television, many advertisements are blatantly sexual, and films are not edited even when they are shown during the day. A high level of violence is also tolerated. The television news will carry explicit coverage of death and injury at any time of day. In a country where so many things were banned, it now seems that anything goes.

The Spanish are usually kind and courteous to the foreigners they meet, but perhaps this is because these foreigners are usually European tourists, who come to spend money in Spain. People of a different color are not so easily accepted. There is also long-standing prejudice and discrimination against the gypsies, who are generally considered to be lawbreakers. While many of them have become part of Spanish society, others continue to lead their traditional nomadic way of life. Gypsies were at one time most numerous in southern Spain, where the flamenco music and dance that they brought with them took root. Large communities now exist in Madrid and Barcelona as well.

RELIGION

Catholicism was the state religion from the Civil War until the Constitution of 1978. Now Spain has no official religion, but the Roman Catholic Church continues to receive financial support from the state. The vast majority of the population is Roman Catholic. Yet, by the 1980s only about 25 percent of Spaniards regularly attended church on Sundays. For

The Cathedral of Barcelona (13th–15th century) is dedicated to the city's patron saint, St. Eulalia.

the others religion plays little part in life beyond the formal occasions of going to church to be baptized, married (often to please older relatives), and buried. However, almost all their customs and traditions have religious roots.

Those following other religions are non-Catholic Christians, a rapidly growing Muslim population (as the number of immigrants increases), and some Jews.

LIVING FOR THE MOMENT

The Spanish are confident, open individuals with a zest for life, and for living every moment, that is contagious. If they invite you somewhere it is because they really want you to come. They do not want you to go home because you are all having such a good time. Who cares about tomorrow? Now is important. While there is a good time to be had, no one will leave quickly. People meet between 10:00 and 11.30 p.m. for dinner, which is followed by relaxed and enjoyable conversation, coffee, and some alcoholic drinks. This is known as *la sobremesa*. During the weekend, night stretches into morning, and you have some breakfast before you go home! You need stamina here, especially if it is *fiesta* time. If there is time, they will snatch a brief *siesta* to prepare themselves for the next night. Partying in Andalusia also requires some training. It never feels like the right time to have a last drink. Instead, someone will suggest *la penúltima*, the last but one, because nobody wants to refer to the end of the evening.

Noise

All this exuberance results in a lot of noise. In 1990 44 percent of Madrid's streets were found to have continuous noise level above the rate considered tolerable by the World Health Organization. Mopeds roar around, and horns are honked all the time. In bars there may be several loud conversations going on amid the sound of slot machines and the ever-popular television in the corner.

Spanish people tend to shout. Everyone wants his or her opinion to be heard, and Spanish can be a harsh-sounding language. In *The Spanish Temper* Victor Pritchett comments "Castilian (Spanish) is above all a language which suggests masculinity, or at any rate it is more suited to the male voice than to the feminine voice which, in Spain, shocks one by its lack of melody."

If you want to try out your Spanish, don't speak quietly, or you may not even be heard. Pope John Paul visited Spain in 1983 and had to say *"El Papa también quiere hablar"* ("The Pope would like to speak too"), to try and silence the large crowd that had gathered. Spaniards do not seem to be able to stop talking for long. It seems that whatever goes through their mind comes out of their mouths. There is no quiet time here, and Spaniards feel uneasy with silence.

> ### They Can't Keep Quiet!
> At the theater one evening, a visitor from
> Andalusia could take the suspense no longer,
> and shouted an urgent warning to one of the
> actors onstage, who was being stalked!

MANNERS

The Spanish people can be quite formal until they
are introduced. After that, the rules are relaxed. Once
you are considered a friend, you will be treated in a
warm and familiar way, and polite formulas will not
be necessary. As is the case in many other countries,
you will find that the manners of the older generation
are usually more formal, and a certain distance should
be maintained. Always, when in doubt, err on the side
of good manners.

Women greet each other and men with a kiss on
both cheeks, or sometimes on one when the person
is a very close relative or friend. Men shake hands,
and they hug close friends, loudly slapping each other
on the back at the same time. Spaniards are generally
very tactile people. They will often touch your arm to
emphasize a point or a joke.

At times, however, to outsiders they may seem
discourteous, or even rude. "Please" and "thank you,"
considered normal among English-speaking people,
and especially the British, are thought to be excessive

and unnecessary among family and close friends, or in everyday exchanges in shops or restaurants. The Spanish language is quite direct. Polite forms and expressions are not often used. In a bar, for example, Spaniards will not say "Could I have coffee please?" but "*Pónme un café, por favor*" ("Give me a coffee, please") or "*Me pones un café?*" ("Would you give me a coffee?), in which "please" is not even needed.

Not only the Spanish language but also the people can be very direct once they get to know you. If you are not looking your best, they will tell you so, not with any offensive intention but with the aim of finding out about the reason or pointing out that you should take care.

This directness has its brighter side. The Spanish are the masters of *piropos* (compliments)—to their friends and to the passer-by. In the market, many vendors refer to or address women as *Princesa* (Princess) and *Reina* (Queen), and on the street Spanish men are not shy about showing their appreciation of the female form. A cheerful "*Hola, guapa!*" ("Hello, gorgeous!") is often to be heard and does not necessarily imply any sign of attraction. Some people like it, others not so much. If the latter is your reaction, try not to be annoyed. If you ignore the comment, that is as far as it goes. Even better, accept the compliment with a smile, and go on your way.

CHAPTER THREE

CUSTOMS
& TRADITIONS

Spain is steeped in customs and traditions that are proudly maintained to preserve regional identity. The year is punctuated by the many *fiestas*, and the participants' energy and enthusiasm makes every holiday an unforgettable experience. Most of the festivals have a religious origin (Holy Week, the pilgrimages, and the many saints' days), although the social aspect has taken over in most cases and many consider them an opportunity to relax or travel. Others are based on historical events or have origins shrouded in the mists of time. On the following pages you will find some of the most important festivals, although there are countless others.

Fiestas can be translated as festivals, public holidays, or just parties. The Spanish are masters of the art of celebrating. Each city, town, and village has its own festival, usually linked to its patron saint, and lasting between a week and a fortnight. Some of these *fiestas* are internationally famous, such as La Semana Santa

(Holy Week) especially celebrated in Andalusia; Los San Fermines, the festival honoring Saint Fermín, famous for the bulls running in the streets of Pamplona; or La Tomatina from Buñol (Valencia), where streets become a crowded battlefield and tomatoes are the weapons.

PUBLIC HOLIDAYS

Twenty years ago Spain seemed to have one day off after another, but everything is more regulated now and some of the religious festivals are no longer considered festive days. Holidays can be divided into four categories: national holidays, applicable everywhere; national holidays that can be replaced in the autonomous communities (political regions); autonomous community (regional) holidays; and holidays of the autonomous communities' capital cities.

The chart opposite shows the national holidays. Each region has its patron saint, and its saint's day is also usually chosen.

If a holiday falls on a Tuesday or a Thursday, people often take an unofficial extra day on the Monday or Friday, giving them a long weekend. This is known as a *puente* (bridge) and is especially common over December 6 and 8. Holidays falling on a weekend are not moved. Most people take their annual vacation in August, and many businesses, especially small to medium-sized enterprises (SMEs), close for the duration.

NATIONAL HOLIDAYS

National holidays have been reduced considerably in recent years.
Today only eight remain:

January 1 New Year's Day

January 6 Epiphany

April * Holy/Good Friday

May 1 May Day/Labor Day

August 15 Feast of the Assumption (not banks)

October 12 Spanish National Day

December 8 Immaculate Conception

December 25 Christmas Day

* Represents a movable date in the months of March and April.
The date depends on the first full moon of spring.

THE FESTIVAL CALENDAR

Some *fiestas* are just days off, while others can be an excuse for a week of carousing, day and night. Here are a few of the best known:

Navidad (Christmas)

Christmas Eve is known as Nochebuen (the Good Night). A lot of people go to *La misa del gallo* (midnight mass), even if they do not attend mass regularly. They will have a big family supper that evening and a long lunch the next day, at which shellfish, fish, turkey, or lamb may be served. Nougat and almond-based cakes are also typical. Most families will have a *belén* (crib) with the holy family, shepherds, and the three kings. Catalonia also has *el caganer*, a traditional figurine who is placed squatting in the corner of the Christmas crib, trousers around his ankles—a mixture of the sacred and profane.

El Tió

In Catalonia, on December 24 children receive presents from *el tió*—a log of wood. The children decorate the log, leave the room, say a prayer, and sing a song to *el tió*. Then they go back in, tap it with a stick, and find presents under a cloth. *El tió* is actually supposed to *cagar* the presents ("deposit them from his rear end" is a polite way of saying it). The first time a group of children explained this tradition to me, they all got extra homework as a punishment for being rude in class! I apologized later.

The magical night, however, is still January 5. Towns hold a parade to celebrate the arrival of the three kings (*los reyes magos*) by horse or camel, attended by their pages, who throw sweets to the children along the way. That night, before bed, children leave food and drink out for the kings and their camels, and they find their presents in the morning. This tradition runs alongside Santa Claus arriving on Christmas Eve, and in some cases children get lucky on both occasions.

Nochevieja

New Year's Eve (Nochevieja) involves another big dinner for family or friends. At midnight the chimes are relayed all over Spain from the Puerta del Sol ("the gate of the sun," the central square in Madrid from which all distances in Spain are measured). Everybody eats twelve grapes, one with each chime. This is to bring you luck in the months ahead. The trick is not to chew, or you will be left with a mouthful of grapes. Just swallow each grape, and go on to the next one! People welcome in the New Year with *cava*, the sparkling wine from Catalonia. After dinner the young people will go out, and may not be back until late the following morning.

San José

St. Joseph's Day, March 19, was once a holiday all over Spain. Now most regions have replaced it with another day. For Valencia, however, it is still important since it coincides with Father's Day and the close of their largest and most spectacular festival, Las Fallas. *Las fallas* are gigantic papier-mâché statues of local, national, and international figures with satire and fantasy as their main themes. The professionals who make the *fallas* (*los artistas falleros*) work on the effigies from the moment the party ends the previous year. They can be as tall as buildings and cost up to a few millions euros to build. At the start of the *fiesta*, March 15, a jury chooses the best *falla*. There is the overall winner, but a second and a third prize are awarded as well, and prizes for originality and interpretation of the traditional giants. A single figure from each Fallas is saved; this is known as the *ninot indultat*. The rest are ceremoniously burned on March 19. There are many street processions of a religious nature. People dress up in traditional costume and offer flowers to their patron saint, the *Virgen de los Desamparados* (the Virgin of the Defenseless). The festivities begin with the sound of hundreds of firecrackers going off, one after another, shaking the walls and leaving a smell of gunpowder in the air. The smell of the gunpowder mixes with the sweet aromas of *churros* (fried dough pastries) with chocolate and *buñuelos* (a regional pastry of the season). By the time the fires light the sky the festival is in full swing.

Carnaval (Carnival)

This is the last fling before the penance and sobriety of Lent—the forty days of fasting and penance before Easter. At Carnaval, anything goes. During the Civil War Franco abolished it in the conquered rebel areas, as the masked participants could not be recognized. After the war there was still a lot of opposition, so Franco banned it again in 1937. Since 1975, however, Carnaval has been back, although it is not a big celebration in all areas. Towns have processions at the weekend either before or after Fat (Shrove) Tuesday. The larger towns have festivities lasting all week. In the Canary Islands Carnaval is celebrated with all the glamor of Rio and its exuberant floats and scanty costumes.

Elaborately costumed reveler at Carnaval.

Cádiz, in Andalusia, also has a very special carnival. As one of Spain's major ports during the sixteenth century, Cádiz copied the carnival of Venice, a city with which it had strong trade links, and since then it has become the liveliest and most dazzling carnival town in mainland Spain, famous for its amusing and creative costumes and satirical song groups. *El Carnaval* was never abolished in Cádiz.

Easter

Easter celebrations begin during Semana Santa (Holy Week), the week preceding Easter. The best-known celebrations take place in Andalusia, although

Good Friday procession depicting the suffering Christ during Holy
Week in Ágreda, Soria.

many other towns throughout Spain have religious
processions at this time. The processions of Castile
(such as at Valladolid and Zamora) are far more austere
than those of Seville or Málaga in Andalusia, where
different processions take place each day, competing
with one another in luxury and splendor.

The parades leave from different churches and wind
slowly around the streets, with their lifelike statues of

Christ on the Cross, and the Virgin Mary in mourning. *Los pasos* (the huge images representing scenes from Christ's last days) are carried or pushed on wheels by members of the *hermandad* or *cofradía* (religious brotherhoods representing trade guilds or other groups).

The participants spend all year preparing the elaborate costumes and decorations. Penitents wear costumes reminiscent of the Ku Klux Klan, having tall hoods with slits for the eyes. In Andalusia people sing *saetas* (heartrending flamenco songs) to the statues from selected balconies. It can all be very moving, although like everything in Andalusia there is a great deal of other noise and festivity going on too.

There is also a tradition, practiced since the Middle Ages, of "passion plays" performed by the locals in several towns. They depict the events leading to Christ's Crucifixion.

Sant Jordi
St. George's Day (April 23) is celebrated in Catalonia, where St. George is the patron saint, and the celebration is the Catalan version of Valentine's Day. Women receive roses and men books—although recently women are becoming more demanding and are asking for a book as well as a rose. The roses represent the one that grew from the blood of the dragon slain by St. George; the books are given because this is the anniversary of the death of Spain's celebrated literary genius, Cervantes. The introduction of giving a book is a recent custom.

Corpus Christi

This feast day, celebrating the Real Presence of Christ in the Eucharist, falls on the first Thursday after Trinity Sunday. In some towns it is a major celebration, usually involving flowers. In the beautiful Andalusian city of Córdoba houses are built in the Moorish tradition. There is little adornment on the outside, but the houses look inward onto courtyards full of flowers, and these private patios are open to all on this day. In Sitges, near Barcelona, some streets are carpeted with patterns made from flower heads, usually carnations.

San Juan

St. John's Eve (June 23), Midsummer's Eve, is a magical night, often celebrated on a beach. There are many associated superstitions. Bonfires are lit, and the tradition in Málaga is to jump over them for luck as they die down. Perhaps the most famous celebration is the "passing of fire" in San Pedro Manrique, in Soria, where the men walk barefoot over a layer of burning embers without suffering any injury. In Ciutadella, on the island of Menorca, they have *caracoleos,* with riders on rearing horses and games reminiscent of medieval times lending a spectacular air to the festivities.

San Fermín

This is the famous *fiesta* where bulls run through the streets of Pamplona, in Navarre, in northern Spain. The week's festival begins officially on July 7, with the ceremony known as El Chupinazo. The mayor addresses the town, and there are fireworks, a lot of shouting, and many bottles of *cava*. The *encierros* (when the bulls are released from their pens outside the town to run to the bullring) take place daily before each bullfight. The bulls dash through the streets, and the locals run ahead of them, distinguished by their white shirts and red sashes. Many outsiders also run, and there are often injuries, which has sparked a debate about safety, alcohol, and the nature of the party. The festivities continue all night long.

PILGRIMAGES AND FAIRS

El Rocío

Andalusia is famous for its *romerías* (pilgrimages) to popular shrines, where *fiestas* are held. Perhaps the most spectacular is the one devoted to *la Virgen del Rocío* (the Virgin of the Dew), popularly

The shrine of *la Virgen del Rocío* is a popular pilgrimage site for millions of visitors.

called el Rocío for short. Nearly a million people from all over Spain make the long journey to gather in the small hamlet of El Rocío in the marshlands of the Guadalquivir River delta, where the statue has been worshiped since 1280. The pilgrims come on horseback and in gaily decorated covered wagons, transforming the area into a colorful and noisy party. The climax of the festival is the weekend before Pentecost Monday. In the early hours of Monday morning the Virgin is brought out of the church to her pilgrims, who all desperately strain to touch the statue. This religious fervor is similar to that shown to the *pasos* (steps) during Semana Santa, and is typical of the Andalusian temperament.

El Camino de Santiago

This has been an internationally famous pilgrimage since the Middle Ages. The apostle James (Santiago) is said to be buried in the town of Santiago de Compostela in Galicia in northwestern Spain, and pilgrims from all over Europe traveled to visit his tomb, coming along *el Camino de Santiago* (the Santiago Way), which runs across the north of Spain. He was named the Patron Saint of Spain by the Catholic Kings, also known as the Kings of the Reconquest, after the expulsion of the Moors. The pilgrimage began to lose popularity in the fourteenth century, and it was not until 1878, when Pope Leo XIII corroborated the authenticity of the remains of the Apostle, that there was a gradual resurgence of pilgrimages. The "Compostela" certificate is awarded to all those who make the pilgrimage for religious reasons, but the pilgrim must show proof of having traveled, on foot, by bicycle, or on horseback, a part of the Pilgrim Road—at least 62 miles (100 km) on foot or horseback, or 124 miles (200 km) by bicycle. This road is now also a favorite route for walkers with no religious motive. The pilgrims pay a token fee to stay in Catholic or local lodges run by charities. The French route is usually the most crowded, especially in summer, and has become quite commercial.

La Feria de Sevilla

This takes place two weeks after Semana Santa and is the first of the *ferias* (fairs) celebrated throughout Andalusia

Visitors to the Feria de Sevilla arrive in horse and carriage, wearing traditional Andalusian dress.

all summer long. The annual *feria* originated in the Middle Ages, when it was the principal means of exchange of local products between towns.

Every town and village in Andalusia has its own *feria*, and it would be possible, if one had superhuman powers of endurance, to spend the whole summer following them about the region. Most other regions have similar *ferias*, generally in August. Different things happen during the day and night. The "day fair" takes place in the streets of the town itself, which is closed to traffic. Businesses close for the week. Tables and chairs are set up, the bars serve food and drink in the street, and music plays on every corner. People of all ages sing and dance, and visitors are welcome.

At night, the fair shifts to the *recinto ferial* (public fairground) on the outskirts of the town. There is a traditional amusement park, with rides for the children, and *casetas* (small marquees) set up by the various clubs, associations, and political parties of the town. Some of these have entertainments, and all have music, room for dancing, and a bar. All night long you will hear the sounds of *sevillanas* (the typical dance) and see the girls dancing gracefully in their traditional long, flounced dresses. Entry to some of the *casetas* is by private invitation only, but there is always a large *Caseta Municipal* put up by the town council and open to everybody.

The *ferias* usually start in the middle of the week and finish on a Sunday night. In the larger towns they start at midnight on a Sunday night with fireworks.

The Monday after the *feria* is often a local holiday to help everyone to recover from the festivities.

Gigantes y Cabezudos

These are "giants" and "bigheads," who parade through the town during *fiestas*, and have done so at least since medieval times. The giants are usually tall, papier-mâché kings and queens on a frame carried by a bearer, who hides himself beneath the robes. The *cabezudos* wear huge, papier-mâché heads to disguise themselves. The band precedes them through the streets and the *gigantes* follow in quite a stately fashion, while the *cabezudos* dance about or run after the children. They

Gigantes twirling to the cathedral bells during San Fermín in Pamplona.

have separate dances that they perform to their own specific music. Many towns have at least one pair of *gigantes*, with several accompanying *cabezudos*.

Dracs, Diables, i Castells

Dragons, devils, and castles sound like elements of a fairy tale, but they are actually the main features of *fiestas* in Catalonia. Fire (*foc*) is an integral part of many traditions, and you should be very careful to keep well back from the parade. The *correfoc* (fire run) takes place in the center of the town as darkness falls, with the participants dressed up as devils dashing through the streets. They run ahead of a dragon, carrying torches and setting off firecrackers and showers of sparks. They chase the onlookers, so everybody wears hats, scarves, and old clothes to protect themselves. The dragon is made up of people disguised under a long piece of cloth, and breathes fire on all (more firecrackers!). The parade usually ends in a small square where everybody jumps up and down, daring to get as near to the dragon as possible. The wildest of these celebrations is *el patum*, which takes place in Berga, in the mountains north of Barcelona.

Castells (castles), however, have nothing to do with fire. They are part of the day festival and are "human towers." People stand on each other's shoulders to form a castle. The groups compete to form different variations. The top person is always a small child (called the *anxaneta*), who scales the human tower,

four or five people high, stands with his or her arm
in the air and then slides down almost immediately.
They go into training from the time they can walk, and
scamper up and down with ease.

La Tomatina

During the Tomatina of Buñol (Valencia), streets become
a crowded battlefield with more than a hundred metric
tons of over-ripe tomatoes as the feared weapons. It is
held on the last Wednesday of August. Thousands of
people arrive from China, Australia, the US, and other
corners of the world expressly for this festival. It might
be the largest food festival worldwide. The success of
this party was such that in 2012 over 50,000 people
joined in the mayhem. This caused several safety and
infrastructural challenges and since 2013 official
ticketing was introduced to limit the capacity of the
battle to only 20,000 people.

Los Moros y Cristianos

The "Moors and Christians" takes place in different
towns to commemorate the battle for the town between
these two sides. After a few days of mock fighting and
street processions, the Christians win.

OTHER CUSTOMS

Birthdays (*cumpleaños*) are a bit different in Spain.
Children still have parties with presents and cake, but

adults are expected to treat people to drinks instead of receiving them. So think hard before you ask a big group to sing "Happy Birthday" to you! Your pockets may be empty by the end of the night.

Santos are "name days" and calendars remind people which day corresponds with which saint. However, as they happen every day they are rarely celebrated, with the exception of those coinciding with a popular patron's day. Someone's *Santo* is celebrated on the day of the saint after whom they were named. For example, if you are José, it is March 19. Some people may actually have more of a celebration on their name day than they do on their birthday, especially if their saint is a well-known one.

"Friday the thirteenth" is not unlucky in Spain. As happens in Greece and some regions of Latin America, in Spain bad luck comes on *martes trece* (Tuesday the thirteenth). There are multiple theories explaining why Tuesday acquired such a bad reputation.

April 1 in Spain is not All Fool's Day. This falls on December 28, *el día de los inocentes* (the day of the [slaughter of the] innocents), and children play tricks (*inocentadas*) on each other.

These are just some of the many customs and traditions of Spain. Every region has its own. Sometimes the best festivals are the smaller ones, as the larger ones can be very crowded and full of tourists. If you can go to a local festival with local people, it will be the experience of a lifetime.

FLAMENCO

Spain is known worldwide for its flamenco music and dancing, which are an important part of many *fiestas*. The *gitanos* (gypsies) are the masters of flamenco, and are presumed to have brought it to Spain. Early flamenco seems to have been purely vocal, accompanied only by rhythmical clapping of hands (*toque de palmas*). The guitar was introduced later. Flamenco was first mentioned in literature in 1774. Between 1765 and 1860, the first flamenco schools were founded at Cadiz, Jerez de la Frontera, and Triana, in Seville.

The "*cante hondo*," the most serious and powerful flamenco singing, was developed during the golden age of flamenco between 1869 and 1910. From 1915 onward flamenco shows were organized and performed all over the world. There was a lull in popularity, but in 1955 a sort of flamenco renaissance began. Outstanding dancers and soloists soon left the small *tablaos* (flamenco clubs) for the great theaters, and guitar players also began to achieve greater recognition.

BULLFIGHTING

Bullfighting is also a part of many *fiestas*. It began in the Middle Ages as a diversion for the aristocracy, when it took place on horseback. By the eighteenth

A matador in action before the arrival of the *picadors* and *banderillos*.

century the poorer population had invented a version on foot. Francisco Romero, who laid down rules for the sport around 1700, is considered the father of bullfighting.

By its fans *la corrida* (the bullfight) is considered an art rather than a sport, technique being very important. It could not exist without the *toro bravo*, a species of bull that is now found only in Spain. There is a strict order to the proceedings. All three matadors and their *cuadrillas* (teams) are introduced to the public, and then the first matador takes his place in the ring.

There are three parts to the *corrida*:

- The matador shows his skill by facing the bull and defending himself only with his cape. He is then joined by the *picadors*, on horseback and armed with lances, who harry the bull.

- Three helpers (*banderilleros*) each stick a pair of *banderillas* (short spears) into the bull's back.

- The bullfighter shows his *faena* (mastery), dominating the bull with his red cape. The *corrida* ends as he kills the bull with his sword.

Bullfighting was banned in Catalonia in 2012. Since then all bullrings of the Autonomous Community have been closed or given a different use. Yet, there have been some signs suggesting a reevaluation of this prohibition.

Apart from bullfighting, bulls are traditionally part of many local festivities taking different forms: *encierro* (runs) as in the San Fermines; *toro embolado*, an evening event when material is attached to the horns of the bull and set on fire; or *bous a la mar*, typically from Denia in Alicante (the Valencian region), where the *encierro* takes place starting at a high point in a village leading to a temporary bull ring next to the sea.

CHAPTER FOUR

MAKING FRIENDS

The Spanish, we have seen, are renowned for their sociability, friendliness, and hospitality. A large part of their leisure time is spent outside the home. You are welcome in their homes but, perhaps because of the great climate, they usually prefer to meet in their favorite bars or restaurants, at all hours of the day and night. They love talking, and will strike up a conversation with anyone. The further south you go, the easier it seems to meet new people.

The climate undoubtedly influences their habits. The summer midday sun is braved only by "mad dogs and Englishmen." Most people rest then, because the cool evening is when everything happens. After work they will usually go first to a local bar to wind down, and then home or to a restaurant for dinner. As some people do not finish work until 8:00 p.m., they may not eat until 10:00 p.m., and dinner may last a couple of hours or more. After which, on the weekend, the night usually continues on at some bar or club, until the early hours of the morning, and sometimes even having breakfast before going back home. Prompting the joke of going home "early." Yet you will be expected to be up early the next day, especially if you work. The Spanish sleep very little as a result of their extended work hours and social life. People with young children, of course, are more home-based, and may not keep such long hours, but the tendency to stay up late is still strong.

So, how do you get to know the Spanish people? If you are working or studying in Spain, start with your colleagues or classmates. After the formality of a first business meeting, you will soon be on friendly terms. The Spaniards usually socialize in big groups of friends or family. Once you become friends with one person you will be asked to come along and join the whole group. You will soon become part of it. However, they will probably not invite you to their homes. Entertaining, as we have seen, usually happens at restaurants. If you are invited to someone's home, take them a good bottle of wine, chocolates, or little pastries. They are not great fans of flowers like other European peoples; they prefer to receive gifts that can be shared.

If you do not manage to find a group of friends through your ready-made contacts, there are other ways. For adults and international students, for instance, there are lots of groups you can join on Facebook where people share hobbies and passions. Signing up for dancing classes or language exchanges are other good ideas.

LANGUAGE CLASSES

In a country where people love talking, it is almost obligatory to learn their language. More people speak English now, especially young people in the larger cities, but traditionally Spaniards have not been very good at foreign languages, and it is a good idea for you to learn some Spanish. A phrase book and a pocket dictionary are good to begin with, but if you plan to stay for a while or will be visiting Spain often, consider doing a basic Spanish course. It will pay dividends. Even if you do not achieve a very high level, any attempt at speaking Spanish will be highly appreciated.

The Instituto Cervantes (www.cervantes.es) is the Spanish equivalent of the British Council, not only teaching the languages—there are four official languages in Spain—but also promoting Spanish culture. It has branches in many other countries as well as in Spain, and these are ideal places to attend classes and find out about Spain before you get there.

When you arrive in Spain you can choose from hundreds of different language centers in cities and towns. You will be assessed and placed in the appropriate level. Classes usually include grammar and speaking practice in a small class (four to ten students). Intensive language courses are recommended to get you started. Four hours of classes daily, for a minimum period of two weeks, should give you some confidence and a basic vocabulary to build on.

There are sometimes excursions and other complementary activities. Fellow students will often have useful tips on how to get to know the locals too. Some schools have Spaniards attending other language classes, and you may see advertisements for people looking for *intercambios* or *tandems* (language exchanges), where you meet informally to help them with English or another language while they help you to perfect your Spanish.

In regions where another language is spoken (the Basque Country, Catalonia, Galicia), a few words of courtesy in the local language will be appreciated, but no one will expect you to learn that language unless you intend to stay in the area for a long time—many locals, especially the younger generations, do not speak them either. Spanish is spoken and understood everywhere, so it makes sense to choose it as your starting point.

EXPATRIATE CLUBS

It is always a good idea to register with your embassy or consulate, which may be able to give you a list of clubs and associations set up by people from your home country. These can vary, from charitable associations to sports or networking clubs and other groups. Even if you have decided to shun people from back home and embrace Spanish culture, these contacts can be a useful source of recommendations about anything from Spanish classes to doctors, dentists, and workmen.

SPORTS AND OTHER GROUPS

Joining others for sports, hobbies, or other common interests is a good way to get to know people—and to practice the language. In the local newspapers, and especially now on social media networks, you will find all types of courses advertised, from cookery to dancing and first aid. Even if you have problems with the language, it is easier to feel confident and comfortable with other people if you are doing something you enjoy and can discuss.

Sports Clubs

Most sports are available in Spain's varied landscape and favorable climate. In the cities there are plenty of gyms, exercise classes, tennis courts, and other sports grounds and facilities. There is usually a joining or membership fee and then an annual or monthly payment. For swimming, there are municipal pools and private clubs in the cities, and swimming competitions to be entered if you are interested. Some gyms also have swimming pools, saunas, and jacuzzis. There are also many golf clubs, especially in the south. Prices vary, and not all are open to the public.

In the winter, skiing and snowboarding in the mountains are very popular. Travel agents can tell you about special deals with ski clubs in the different winter resorts. Yet winter sports in general are not that culturally rooted among the Spaniards. At present, running is very popular.

THE NEIGHBORS

Try to use the same shops, bars, and restaurants in your locality. People will get to know you, and you will be able to practice speaking with them. The Spanish are used to buying bread every day; bread is to Spaniards what pasta is to Italians. There are bakeries everywhere where you will find lots of sweet and savory specialties and, of course, the distinctive Spanish bread. Their traditional bread is similar to the French baguette, but thicker. Ask for a *barra de cuarto*, *pan de pueblo*, or *pan de chapata*. You will soon become one of the locals if you follow their example.

Everyone has a favorite bar where they have breakfast, coffee during the day, and probably a *copita* (little drink) on the weekend or on Friday after work.

Cafés and bars are popular venues for meeting up with friends.

Bar staff are used to chatting to the customers, so ask them for information—appeal to their love of their region to find out the best places to see, to visit, and to shop. And be prepared to do your bit by answering their questions about your own country and traditions too.

ENGLISH-LANGUAGE PUBLICATIONS

There are also many English-language newspapers and magazines in Spain. The following is a selection from different areas: *Barcelona Metropolitan* (monthly); *The Broadsheet* (monthly, throughout Spain); *Guidepost* (weekly, Madrid); *Majorca Daily Bulletin* (daily); *Lookout* (quarterly, Costa del Sol); *Island Connections* (fortnightly, Canary Islands); *Sur in English* (weekly, Málaga).

CHAPTER **FIVE**

THE SPANISH AT HOME

Today most Spaniards live in towns or cities, chiefly in Madrid and in the coastal towns. Only 53 percent of the population lived in towns in 1953, but by 1980 this had risen to 75 percent. The figure has varied very little since then. Recently, however, as a result of the financial crisis, some families have moved back to the villages in search of a more affordable lifestyle.

SPANISH HOMES

The majority of Spaniards in cities and large towns live in apartments (*pisos*). An apartment may be a huge property on one of the nation's most exclusive streets, or a modest, three-bedroomed affair in a high-rise block. The older buildings traditionally had a caretaker (*conserje*), who lived on the ground floor and kept an eye on things, but there are very few of these left now.

In many of the smaller towns and villages people live in a type of house that has been popular for several years. It is a small, three-story house with the living area on the upper two floors and a garage on the ground floor. There is not always a garden, although those houses that come with one often have a swimming pool too.

In rural areas people live in houses that vary greatly from one area to another. Local stone is used, and each area has its particular style. In Andalusia, houses are built around beautiful patios, reflecting the influence of Moorish architecture.

Andalusian houses are designed around an internal courtyard.

In Spain more people own a second home than in any other country in the European Union. Perhaps this is partly because many who left their villages and towns to work in the larger towns and cities did not sell their family homes. Every weekend city-dwellers leave the cities in droves to go to their village homes (known as chalets) or little apartments outside the city. Outside Madrid and other major cities you will see complexes (*urbanizaciones*) of these apartments with swimming pools, tennis courts, sports clubs, supermarkets, and everything that is needed to make them the perfect vacation home. Many families spend their summer vacations here while the father remains in the city, joining them on weekends. Others travel between their vacation home and job every day.

In the past there were very few rental properties, compared to other European countries. This was due to government policies rather than choice. Franco froze rents in 1936 and allowed tenants to pass on their leases to any relatives living with them at the time of their death. It was not until the 1980s that the government altered the legislation to allow landlords to raise rents in accordance with the cost of living, and some tenants are still paying a pittance, even in very expensive areas. Because landlords could not sign a new, up-to-date lease with the occupants, they were very wary of new tenants and would often insist on one-year contracts. It is difficult to evict a troublesome tenant. However, the situation is changing as long or permanent job contracts are now less common, and people tend to move between cities in search of work. As a result, the rental business is flourishing, and finding short- or medium-term rentals can be very challenging due to the high demand. Since a quarter of the population owns a second property, many of these are now available to rent. The cost of housing, and the lack of rental property, is one reason why Spaniards live at home until they buy their own apartment— usually when they marry.

Although the government has helped with subsidized housing and low-interest loans, most of this housing is, and always has been, for sale, not for rent. Prices have never been cheap, and thus the poorest people, who continue to rent, have been kept out of the housing market altogether.

THE HOUSEHOLD

Spanish culture has traditionally been dominated by men. The man was in charge of sustaining the family financially and the woman took care of the home and raising children. Although this might still be true for some rural areas and traditional families, it would no longer be valid to associate Spanish men and women with these gender roles. The reality today is more complicated. Since women were incorporated into the working world, they have been pursuing greater equality in all areas, whether in the household, salaries, politics, or higher management roles.

However, full equality has not yet been achieved and surveys still confirm that women, whether they work outside the home or not, spend more time than men on domestic duties.

Spanish women are extremely house-proud, and although many apartment complexes may look neglected from the outside, they will be sparkling inside. Children are taught to be helpful around the house, although in some families the sons are still excused. This is again a question of values and customs. Some men do help in the house or even share the work more or less equally with their female counterparts, but women still do the lion's share. In Catalonia, *fer dissabte* (to do Saturday) refers to the extra cleaning done on a Saturday when there is more time.

In all parts of Spain people eat a Mediterranean diet. Said to be one of the healthiest diets in the world, it includes plenty of fruit, vegetables, fish, meat, and, of course, olive oil. It will differ from one region to another, depending on what is available locally. People use fresh produce whenever possible, and regard pre-prepared food as inferior. In a Spanish apartment complex the smell of cooking is pervasive from early morning, as intricate dishes are prepared.

The mother traditionally used to hover around the table, clearing one course away to produce the next, and eating when she could. However, as more women join the workforce and fewer grandmothers are living nearby to help, this is changing. People do cook meals

Fresh herbs, tomatoes, garlic, and olive oil are standard ingredients in Spanish cuisine.

from scratch, if necessary starting the cooking the previous evening and finishing it on the following day, but this involves a great deal of work, and most working women are now cutting down where they can on the hours spent in the kitchen.

Despite this traditional healthy diet and varied cuisine, Spanish people have a weight problem, and in recent years Spain has become one of the European countries with the highest indexes of obesity. The appetite of young people for fast food and snacks is probably a contributing factor. As a result, dieting centers and gyms have proliferated.

THE DAILY SHOPPING

Most small shops open from 9:00 a.m. to 1:00 or
2:00 p.m., and close for the *siesta*. They reopen from
5:00 p.m. to 8:00 p.m. Larger stores, especially in the
cities, usually stay open all day. Shops in some towns
have Monday closing or may open only half the day
on Saturdays. Tourist areas may have a very different
timetable, staying open late at night when people are
home from the beach and out for an evening stroll.
Some of them are even allowed to open all year.

Fitches of Iberico ham in a Barcelona market hall.

A fisherman stacks crates of freshly caught sardines.

Some Spaniards still do their shopping daily in local shops and will have a favorite butcher and baker and a preferred fruit and vegetable stand at the local market. However, this habit has been largely replaced by shopping at one of the big supermarkets. Spanish fishmongers will do everything except cook the fish, and butchers will cut, skin, slice, and prepare to order.

All big towns have a covered market, where there is a large selection of fresh produce. There will also usually be an open-air market once a week, with stands selling clothes and kitchen utensils as well as food. The stands are usually no cheaper than the local stores, and are probably not the place to find great bargains. Those who prefer to shop here drive a hard bargain and make the sales assistants earn their money. Sometimes the gypsies will bargain, but never for food. Prices are set.

The Spanish do not usually stand in line, although the storekeepers seem always to know whose turn it is. In some small shops and supermarkets there is a system of tickets that assigns customers their turn according to their arrival time—you take a ticket and wait for your number to be called before being served.

Every town has an emergency twenty-four-hour pharmacy (*farmacia de guardia*) service. In most cases you will not have access to the interior of the pharmacy and a pharmacist will assist you from a special counter with bulletproof glass. Do not draw hasty conclusions; everybody likes to feel safe when working late at night.

If you need to arrange a transaction or talk to someone from your bank, try to be there before 2:00 or 3:00 pm. Although this is starting to change for some banks, most of them close to the public at that time—and they do not open on the weekend. Bank transfers take between two and three working days (*días laborables* or *hábiles*). So if you do the transaction on a Friday it is possible that the money will not reach its intended recipient until Tuesday or Wednesday. Additionally, be aware that most banks charge a fee for withdrawals at another bank's ATM, so it pays to find the closest ATM of your own bank.

DAILY LIFE

Despite staying up late, most Spaniards start the day early, at 7:00 or 8:00 a.m. Breakfast at home can be quite perfunctory, as most people prefer to have a sandwich or pastry later in the morning, in a light meal called *almuerzo*. This usually involves a trip to the local bar, where the waiters will be kept frenetically busy for an hour or so. The most extended *almuerzo* consists of coffee with milk, a croissant, or toast with fresh tomato, olive oil and salt, or jam, and a glass of freshly squeezed orange juice. Bread could be *de bocadillo* (baguette-like) or *de sándwich* (the American, milky white square slices). Although not all bars and restaurants have it yet, you can try asking for soya, lactose-free, or skinny milk. The trendier the bar is, the higher the probability of finding these alternatives.

Between 1:00 and 2:00 p.m. most people leave work and head home for their lunch around 2:00 p.m. Traditionally, lunch is followed by a nap—the famous *siesta*—but, because most people now commute further between home and work, this custom has practically disappeared and is left for the weekends. The main daily television news is broadcast at this time, as are some of the most popular programs, including the melodramatic *culebrones* (soap operas) from South America and national TV series.

Most businesses close around 8:00 p.m., but shops are another story. From the close of business the bars start buzzing with people having a *cervecita* or *caña* (little beer) before going home. The evening meal will be after 9:00 p.m. It will be lighter than the midday meal, and will be eaten out or at home with the family. People will often stay up until well past midnight, and in the summer you may see them sitting outside their houses *tomando el fresco* (enjoying the cool air) and passing on the local news. Although the Spanish are extremely friendly, they do not readily invite people to their homes—socializing is done outside the home. Even teenagers are more likely to meet at the local *plaza* (square) than in one of their bedrooms.

The Online Generation

Social networks are no longer just reserved for grown-ups. They have also had a significant impact on how the young socialize. Kids and teenagers are constantly connected to social media and most of the time interact with each other via these platforms, even while being together. Recent studies have shown a negative impact of social media usage on young people's social skills, empathy, and the way they perceive relationships. Certain networks such as *Facebook* have lost much of their popularity among their youngest users and have been replaced by platforms such as Instagram and Musical.ly, where users portray themselves and share their activities constantly. This has become a serious concern for parents, who worry about their children's privacy, health, and safety.

EDUCATION

Education is very important for the Spanish. It is worth noting that the translation of the word "polite" is *bien educado*, well educated. Education is a means of bettering oneself. There has always been a feeling that one's children should do something better than manual labor, and the majority of Spanish parents want their children to go on to a college or university.

Just under half the children in Spain attend private schools. These are now almost all state-funded, and range from exclusive, bilingual educational

Children are obliged to start school at the age of six, though many attend early education institutes from the age of three.

establishments to schools where the teachers may have no other recommendation than being related to the principal. Public schools are controlled more strictly by the state. Until recently there were two types of school: BUP (Bachillerato Unificado Polivalente), leading to university, and FP (Formacion Profesional), leading to manual jobs. However, education is now compulsory until the age of sixteen, and all children go to one type of school. New subjects have been introduced in an attempt to bring about changes in traditional thinking (environmental conservation, peace studies, sexual equality), languages are taught earlier, from seven or eight years of age, and the emphasis is on confidence building, although the final exams have stayed more or less the same.

Children usually attend school from three years of age, although it is not obligatory until the age of six. They have a very long day. Primary school begins at 9:00 a.m. and ends at 2:00 p.m. Although there are some regions, such as the Valencian Community, that still follow the old schedules. This means having a break at 1:00 or 2:00 p.m and continuing from 3:00 to 5:00 p.m. After that, many children go on to extracurricular activities such as foreign language studies or sports, and also to do their homework.

Most families have dinner together, but younger children have an early supper around 8:00 p.m. They also have a snack between 5.00 and 7.00 p.m. called *merienda* (tea time). Most teenagers eat with their parents and also go to bed late, having fitted homework and other activities into the evening.

In the past many students worked in the mornings and studied in the evenings, or *vice versa*. There was no time limit for finishing a course, so people would stay at college for as long as necessary. Students once had to go to their local university, but may now choose where to study. There is still a shortage of places and grants as there are many young people, better educated than before, competing for them. However, this will probably change in the future as the Spanish birth rate has decreased from one of the highest in Europe to one of the lowest.

TELEVISION

In summer the Spaniards spend a lot of time out of doors, but in winter some watch a great deal of television—more than three hours a day. In some families, even when no one is watching it, the television is often left on. The quiz "Saber y Ganar" ("Knowing and Winning") has been running daily on the Spanish public TV channel (TVE) and with the same presenter since 1997, so jokes and memes arise from time to time regarding things that change in life and others that stay the same, like this program. In recent years, Spanish serials and reality TV shows in the areas of cooking, singing, and other talent competitions have become enormously popular among young both people and adults. In fact, most of the contestants representing Spain in the Eurovision Song Contest were public favorites or winners of these shows. Nevertheless, Spanish television, sometimes referred to as *la caja tonta* (the silly box), has lost popularity with the rise of digital platforms such as Netflix, HBO, and Amazon.

There are two national channels—TVE1 and TVE2. Some autonomous regions also have their own channels, often broadcasting in the local language or dialect, but these vary in quantity and quality. Private channels have existed since late 1989, and they have multiplied since the introduction of digital satellite television. The competition has lessened the public television's advertising revenue. In 2014 Televisión Española (TVE) stopped broadcasting commercials, and as a result, government funding has had to be increased. TVE has also several radio stations, as well as the national orchestra and choir.

In 2014, official sources showed that Spanish political views are greatly influenced by what people see on television. Since then, televised debates between the candidates of the major political parties have become the norm and they coexist, especially in the election season, with plenty of other debates, interviews, documentaries, and discussion programs of a political nature.

In recent years, however, social media has been shown to have an even greater influence on people's political views. Some reports on this phenomenon estimate that around 30 percent of the population's votes are influenced by social media. Naturally, politicians follow this trend and are therefore extremely active on social networks during election times, and actively maintain their online presence between elections. They are also concerned about fake news and the impact of misinformation on the votes cast for their parties. Social media seems to have replaced television as the main channel of (mis) information among politicians, the general public, and young people in particular.

THE PRESS

The Spanish do not buy as many newspapers as people in other European countries, and with the rise of online newspapers many think that the printed form will disappear. Yet, most bars provide newspapers for their clients, and it would be difficult to calculate how many people read any one newspaper. In general, Spain has quality newspapers and nothing equivalent to the tabloids and gutter press of other countries. The daily sports papers *AS*, *Marca,* and *Superdeporte* are very popular. The main national newspapers are *El Pais, ABC, El Mundo, La Razon,* and *Publico.*

There are, however, a large number of magazines covering all interests. *Hola!*, established in 1944 is avidly read and is based on photos and interviews with society figures and the *farándula* (celebrities). In 1988 an English version, *Hello!,* was launched.

The end of censorship during the transition from the Franco dictatorship led to a totally different type of magazine, *Interviú*, which "set out to provide its readers with the two things they had been denied under Franco—uninhibited coverage of politics and pictures of naked women," comments John Hooper in *The New Spaniards*. The magazine contains interviews with politicians, interspersed with sexy photos. For the non-Spanish reader its full-color features, which have explicit shots of killings and accidents, can be shocking.

The ubiquitous newsstands display the huge range that is available—history, business, science, nature, sports, cars. Spaniards may not buy many newspapers, but that does not mean they do not read.

CHAPTER SIX

TIME OUT

Spanish sociability is legendary. Free time is spent with friends and family, and most people are out more often than they are at home. As they say, "*Viven en la calle*" ("They live in the street"). Most working women and young couples, especially if they have children, devote Saturday mornings to housework or going to the supermarket to get ready for the next week. Their other preferred activities are shopping, making family visits, playing or watching sports, or meeting up with friends. Sundays are often the day for visiting the closest family and sharing lunch with them. Many people who live in the cities have second homes on the coast or in the mountains, usually in the same region as their permanent residence, where they spend their weekends and holidays. This is especially true for Valencians, Catalans, or Andalusians who like to enjoy the coast and the good weather all year. The resulting traffic jams back into major cities on Sunday evenings are best avoided.

SHOPPING FOR PLEASURE

As in many other countries, in Spain shopping is a popular pastime as well as a necessity. In the cities you will find fashion boutiques, shopping malls, and the Spanish department store El Corte Inglés. These centers are usually open between nine or ten in the morning and nine or ten in the evening. Sunday opening is not consistent throughout the country. In some areas stores will open only for three or four Sundays a year, mainly around Christmas time, while others are open throughout the year. Smaller shops, especially in small towns or outside the city center, may close for a several hours for lunch.

Mercados and *mercadillos* (markets and little markets) of every nature are very popular in Spain, and there are open-air and covered markets in most towns. On weekends you will find flea markets, with an abundance of knickknacks, collectibles, and crafts.

The most famous of these street markets is the huge Sunday morning *rastro* that takes place in the center of Madrid, and is well worth a visit. There are many stands to browse through, and as you walk around the streets you will find plenty of bars open for breakfast, brunch, or lunch.

Valencia has the biggest fresh food market of Europe. The covered Mercado Central (Central Market) was also the first market worldwide to computerize sales and introduce home deliveries.

The counter of this bar in Madrid offers a tempting array of different *tapas*.

EATING OUT

It is a widespread custom to go for a *tapa* or *pincho* (or *pintxo,* if you are in the Basque region) before meals. These snacks are often smaller-sized versions of proper meals, served over a slice of bread in the case of *pinchos*, and are the ideal way to taste unusual dishes. There are hundreds of different *tapas*, but a few typical ones are *buñuelos de bacalao* (cod croquettes), *champiñones al ajillo* (mushrooms in garlic sauce), *tortilla de patatas* (Spanish potato omelette), *pescadito frito* (small fried fish), and *pulpo a la gallega* (octopus

123

in paprika sauce). Spaniards will often go to several different bars, tasting the *tapas* and drinking a glass of wine or a small glass of beer (a *caña*) in each one. In Andalusia, particularly, people usually stand at the bar, and do not stay for longer than one or two *tapas* in any one place. And in Madrid you will often get a *pincho* or *tapa* free when ordering a *caña*.

You may notice that some of the best bars look rather scruffy, with a lot of small papers and nutshells all over the floor. This is because, especially when standing, the custom is to throw the tiny paper napkins on the floor on finishing one's *tapa*. This is not considered impolite or a sign of a lack of respect, and it is not that the staff have been neglectful. A bar with a messy floor has a large clientele, and is therefore likely to be good.

In tourist areas the bars will often have menus with photographs of the dishes to avoid language problems. Generally these are not the best places to sample authentic Spanish gastronomy. There will usually be *platos combinados*—big portions of food with many things served on one plate. Eating outside on the *terraza* is very popular, especially in beach or garden settings, but it is worth noting that you will probably have to pay a little more for such prime positions.

The Spanish love eating. They have lunch late in the day, and take their time over a meal. In tourist areas the restaurants will cater to the eating habits of foreigners and open earlier, but elsewhere they do not expect their clients to want lunch before 2:00 p.m., and dinner will not happen until 9:00 or 10:00 p.m. All restaurants usually open for both lunch and dinner, and serve three-course meals at both, although people usually eat less at dinner than at lunch, except perhaps on weekends or when they are on vacation.

There are all kinds of eating-places to experience, from small, family-run bars to large, expensive restaurants, and you can eat well in any of them—the best food is not necessarily to be found at the most expensive restaurants. Spaniards enjoy their food and are knowledgeable about their local dishes, often traveling to restaurants off the beaten path for regional specialties. They will want you to try these specialties, expecting that you will appreciate them too.

In the popular restaurants overworked waiters run between tables, but you will not have to wait too long. At lunchtime there is the *menú del día* (set menu of the day), usually offering two or three courses of a selection of dishes at a modest price. To choose from the more expensive *à la carte* menu, ask for the *carta*. The variety of dishes is often amazing.

On Sundays the *merenderos* (reasonable roadside restaurants) are usually full of big family parties. *Chiringuitos* (the seaside version) are as near to the beach as possible. Bars selling food will be open from early morning until late at night. Much of the food is quite elaborate, and needs a lot of gentle cooking.

Bread is always served although you will not normally find either bread plates or butter on the table. It is served on its own or with fresh tomato rubbed over it. It is customary to ask for olive oil and salt to be brought with your bread. Water is not usually brought unless you ask for it, and then it will be bottled. Drink it from the water glass— larger than the wine glass.

FOOD AND DRINK

Spanish cooking varies greatly from region to region. Mediterranean and Cantabrian cuisine is considered to be the most elaborate and prestigious. Spanish food is often thought to be very spicy, but this is not the case; in general the most piquant ingredient is paprika. The most widely eaten meat is pork (*cerdo*), very often in the form of *fiambre* or *embutido* (cold or dry meat), but in much of the country lamb (*cordero*), or big and tender beef steaks (*solomillo* or *entrecot de ternera*) are eaten on special occasions. Spaniards have long consumed large and assorted amounts of fish (*pecado*) and seafood (*marisco*). Legumes, especially lentils (*lentejas*), chickpeas (*garbanzos*), and white and red beans (*alubias*) also form an important part of the diet.

Every region has its specialty. Around the coast it is usually fish. In Málaga it is the small fish— *pescaditos, sardinas, boquerones*—while in the north (especially Galicia and the Basque Country) the seafood is wonderful—*pulpo a la gallega* (octopus), and *txangurro* (Basque spider crab), and *bacalao al pil-pil* (cod fried in garlic and served in the sauce) are only a few examples. There are many different casseroles (*guisos* or *latos de cuchara*, literally, "spoon dishes"). These are also known as *comida de pobres* (the meals of poor people), since some tend to be cheap to prepare and fill you up. Valencia has *paella,* one of Spain's most famous dishes: saffron-flavored rice with vegetables and seafood, or chicken and rabbit. Valencian people are very

A seafood *paella* cooked on an open fire.

strict and demanding about this dish, and are easily outraged when restaurants or *guiris* (Spanish term for tourists) add pepper, chorizo, chilly, or any other odd ingredient not part of the traditional recipe. They often argue that "rice with things is not *paella.*"

Inland, they serve meat. A traditional meat and vegetables stew is found in Madrid (*cocido madrileño*), Catalonia (*escudellà*), and Andalusia (*potaje*). Meat, legumes, and vegetables are stewed and served in three courses: first the broth, then the vegetables, and finally the meat. In central Spain *cordero* (lamb), *cochinillo* (suckling pig), and *jamones* (cured hams) are the specialties. In Catalonia there is a wonderful variety of cold meats and sausages (*butifarra*), less spicy than the *chorizo* (paprika sausage) from the south. There are many, many more dishes, including, of course, the famous *gazpacho Andaluz*, the cold tomato and garlic soup, and *gazpacho Manchego* (a casserole made with meat, vegetables, and thin wheat tortillas)

Garlic and olive oil are widely used in Spanish cuisine, and everywhere you will see cured hams hanging from the roof or waiting to be sliced behind the bar. These hams are the famous *jamón serrano* or *ibérico* and they are a delicacy prized above ordinary ham (*jamón de York*). There are various classes of this ham that vary in price depending on their quality: *jamón ibérico de bellota* or *de pata negra* are surely a great bet.

TIPPING

The Spanish hardly ever tip. Some expensive restaurants may add a service charge of 10 to 15 percent. Smaller restaurants and bars do not. If you feel the service has been particularly good, you can round up the bill to the next euro or leave a few extra coins out of the change. Spanish people are quite demanding, so they will often not hesitate to let the waiter know that the service or the food was not as it should have been or as good as the last time they visited. Service is expected to be reasonably quick and food always fresh and properly presented. There are no excuses when it comes to food. In the bigger cities, however, tourists may be expected to be more generous spirited than the locals.

With people who provide a service, such as cab drivers, hairdressers, and barbers, it is usual to round up the bill with a few coins.

TABLE MANNERS

Table manners are not very different from those in other Western countries, but the following are worth noting:

- Keep both hands in view above the table. It is not considered polite to rest one hand on your lap while eating with the other.

- It is not polite to put something into your mouth and then take it out again, talk at the same time, or to chew with your mouth open. Therefore, people break off pieces of their bread, rather than bite into it. You can break the bread by hand.
- Prawns can be picked up with the fingers to be eaten, although in expensive restaurants it is recommended to use your cutlery.
- The Spanish hold the fork in the left hand and the knife in the right, and do not switch them. Food is pushed on to the fork with the knife.
- When you have finished, place your knife and fork side by side on the plate.
- If you are just having a pause, place your cutlery on the plate in a triangle.
- To signal that the meal was excellent, place them parallel to each other and to the table edge with the handle to the left side.
- If you found the meal disappointing, cross them over the plate.
- People usually wipe their mouths with their napkin before drinking.
- A typical toast will consist of the host raising his or her wineglass and saying, "*Salud*!"

Alcohol

The best-known red wines (*vino tinto*) come from Rioja, Ribera del Duero, and Navarra in the north. Rioja wines became world-famous when French vineyards suffered from an epidemic of phylloxera in the seventies. The top

Vino tinto, robust red wines come vineyards in the areas of Ribera del Duero and Navarra in northern Spain.

white wines (*vino blanco*) are from Rueda and Penedés in Catalonia and Rias Baixas in Galicia. As you get to know Spanish wines you will also discover a whole range of lesser-known wines as well as the brandies, the *pacharán* (Basque and Valencian regions), the sparkling *cava* (Catalonia), and sherry (Jerez). Sherry is fortified with grape spirit and classified according to type—the pale, delicate *fino*, through *manzanilla*, *amontillado*, and *oloroso*, to the dark, rich and fragrant *palo cortado*. You will find the Andalusians themselves enjoying their crisp, chilled *fino* or *manzanilla* at fiesta time. There is also *sidra* (cider) in Asturias, *Agua de Valencia* (a Valencian cocktail made from a base of champagne or *cava*, vodka, and gin with the added flavor of fresh orange juice), and *sangría* (a kind of wine punch) throughout the country. Spain also produces beer, but this is not usually drunk with meals. It can be ordered at the bar with *tapas*.

To end a meal, many will order a *chupito de licor de hierbas* (a small glass of herb liquor) or a *Pedro Ximenez* or *Muscat* (two varieties of very sweet wines from Andalusia and the Mediterranean). Ordering a coffee, however, is even more common. Perhaps it will be a *café solo* (espresso), a *cortado* (espresso with milk), or a *bombón* (a *cortado* made with *leche condensada*—thick and sweetened milk); you may also like to try a *carajillo*, which is coffee laced with brandy or the spirit of your choice. Just ask for a *carajillo de* . . . (Baileys, for instance). "*Salud*!"

On the weekends, young people meet friends in parks and squares for a drink, This custom is called *botellón* (colloquially, big bottle) and has become popular among the youth as a way to avoid the high prices charged by nightclubs on alcohol. There is some drunkenness but it is a comparatively minor problem. The Spanish do not like to lose their dignity: they drink, but not so much that they are out of control. Perhaps it is precisely because there is so much alcohol around. Most homes have wine on the table, and children may drink it (heavily watered down) from an early age. In some areas the *porró* (a glass carafe with a long spout that you hold up and aim at your mouth) will be in the center of the table for you to help yourself—not an easy thing to do! Things may be changing, but it is still the minority that drinks to get drunk.

NIGHTLIFE

Bars in Spain are open all day and late into the night, most closing by 2:00 or 3:00 a.m., but then there are always the *discotecas* (nightclubs) to move on to. Many of these are free for women before a certain time. Otherwise, the entrance fee will usually include one free drink, but further drinks will be much more expensive than in a bar. The *discotecas* usually close at 5:00 a.m., when people go on for hot chocolate and *churros* (rather like donuts) before going home.

You can also visit a *tablao*—a flamenco club. Andalusia is the home of flamenco, but as the Andalusians moved around, so did their music, and there are now *tablaos* all over Spain—although they tend to be less authentic. The *gitanos* (gypsies) are still the greatest exponents of flamenco. Tourists throng the well-advertised shows, which have troupes of smoldering dancers with long, flounced dresses and castanets. However, the locals will probably go to a much smaller place where the artistes may be older, less easy on the eye, and less acrobatic, but they will have *arte* (the natural skill), and that is all that matters.

CULTURAL ACTIVITIES

The local tourist offices and their Web sites will provide you with a wealth of information on tourist services, local museums, galleries, and other places of interest, and on current events. Also, in Madrid and Barcelona,

the magazine *La Guiá del Ocio* will tell you everything
that is currently going on in those cities. Smaller towns
announce their local events in the newspapers.

The Spanish may not all be frequent visitors of
museums and art galleries, but they do appreciate
and value *cultura* (culture). Most people have a basic
knowledge of artists and art history, especially that
which is relevant to their country and local area.

Museums and Galleries

These are also listed in the entertainment guides. It is
worth noting that most are closed on Mondays. The
state museums are free to Spanish nationals, but some
have free admission on Sundays for everyone. Madrid
boasts the enormous Prado museum, which houses

Designed by Canadian-American Frank Gehry, the Guggenheim Museum Bilbao is a magnificent example of groundbreaking twentieth-century architecture.

paintings by El Greco, Goya, and Velasquez, among many others. Picasso's famous *Guernica* can be seen in the nearby Museo Nacional Centro de Arte Reina Sofía. In Barcelona there are the Museu Picasso and the Fundació Joan Miró, and Bilbao is the site of the Guggenheim Museum, worth a visit to see the building alone. The major national museums are in the large cities, but many smaller Spanish towns often have interesting museums that cover their local history, arts, crafts, and traditions.

Historic Buildings and Antiquities

Spain is full of historic places to visit. There are numerous monumental remains of the Roman occupation to be seen throughout the country: the city walls of Lugo, the aqueducts at Segovia and Tarragona, the theater and public buildings at Mérida, the bridges at Alcántara and Córdoba, and the towns of Italica and Ampurias (Emporion) are all prime examples. There is also an example of an Iberian settlement at Ullastret, in Catalonia. Andalusia has Moorish remains such as the Mezquita (mosque-cathedral) of Córdoba, the Alhambra palace of Granada, and the Alcázar (fortress) of Seville. Every city has its old part, and there are some towns, such as Toledo, Salamanca, and Cuenca, where nearly every building seems worthy of mention. Barcelona's open-air Poble Espanyol is laid out as a small town—you walk through the streets and see replicas of famous buildings from different parts of Spain. You can appreciate the various architectural styles of Catalonia, then turn a corner to see a model of the Giralda in Seville.

Many tourists come to Valencia especially to visit their "City of Arts and Sciences," a cutting-edge cultural complex inspired by nature and designed by the world-famous Valencian architect Santiago Calatrava.

In cathedrals and other places of worship, people are expected to dress modestly (covering legs and arms) and behave respectfully.

Theater, Opera, Dance, and Music

The Spanish love to go to the theater. All cities have several theaters, and many towns also have small ones where local companies perform. Opera and dance can be seen in the cities, and Spain is now on the concert trail of most international stars. The Spanish attitude toward most cultural events is quite relaxed, and people do not dress very formally, except for the opera.

Theaters put on a variety of productions ranging from the classical Golden Age plays of Calderón de la Barca and Lope de Vega to Lorca's twentieth-century dramas *Bodas de sangre*, *Yerma*, or *La Casa de Bernarda Alba*, or translations of international hits such as

One of the several striking buildings in Valencia's "City of Arts and Sciences" cultural complex, designed by Santiago Calatrava.

Germans de Sang, the Catalan version of *Blood Brother*s by Willy Russell, or *Arte (Art)* by Yasmina Reza.

Spain has made a lasting contribution to the world of opera and song with the well-loved Spanish tenors Plácido Domingo and José Carreras, and the soprano Montserrat Caballé, who are all internationally famous. You will find the classical operas occasionally performed, and there is also *zarzuela,* "light" opera similar to the operettas of Johann Strauss or the works of Gilbert and Sullivan.

Dance encompasses both *ballet español* (a mix of ballet and flamenco) and classical ballet, with dancers and directors Victor Ullate and Nacho Duato. Flamenco itself also has its internationally famous exponents, such as the dancer Joaquín Cortes and the guitarist Paco de Lucia.

The most famous Spanish composers are Enrique Granados, Isaac Albéniz, Manuel de Falla, and Joaquín Rodrigo. Andrés Segovia is considered the father of classical guitar.

The major cities all have festivals of theater and music, either over the summer months or integrated into the celebrations of their patron saint. Madrid has its festival in May, with both local and international stars. In Barcelona the Grec in July and August brings many international stars to the city.

Pop Music

Today, Enrique Iglesias (whose father Julio enthralled a previous generation) is one of the best-known pop stars internationally. In Spain there are many groups, but few are known outside the country. Los 40 Principales is the main pop–rock radio station and plays national and international hits, mainly targeting teenagers.

Pop idol Enrique Iglesias enjoys fame in Spain and with audiences abroad.

TV programs such as the reality and talent shows "Operación Triunfo," "La Voz," "X Factor," or "Tú si que valets" are very popular. In 2003, during the final of "Operación Triunfo," it was noted at one point that more than fifteen million people were glued to their screens—a record in Spanish broadcasting history.

Cinema
The cinema, of course, is hugely popular. Most of the films shown are American, and they are often dubbed into Spanish. Original version cinemas, where the films are not dubbed, are getting more popular, but

you will find them only in the cities. They will be marked "v.o." (*versión original*) in the newspapers. The home-produced films are well worth watching if your Spanish is good enough to follow them. In the summer some small towns will show films in the local *plaza* (square). When it starts getting dark you will see people heading to the square carrying chairs under their arms, although some seating may be supplied. The films will be in Spanish, but the atmosphere is great.

Spanish cinema in general is relatively unknown internationally, although the films of the director

Luis Buñuel, full of dark surrealism, anarchy, and wit, have captivated generations of cinemagoers since the late1920s. Today actors such as Antonio Banderas, Penélope Cruz, and Javier Bardem are famous, as is Spain's best-known director, Pedro Almodóvar, who was the most internationally successful member of *la movida*

Acclaimed international actress Penélope Cruz.

madrileña (the Madrid "scene") of the 1980s. This term describes the new artistic activity and atmosphere during the transition from Franco's dictatorship to democracy. The "scene" centered on the nightclubs, where people congregated until the early hours and brought together many new young music groups and people involved in other arts. It has sometimes been compared to London's "swinging sixties."

It used to be said that Spanish cinema is always about the same topics: sex, old-fashioned comedies, the Spanish Civil War, and kitchen-sink dramas. However, in recent years the film industry has successfully reconnected with its public with high quality productions. Other famous names in the industry are Alejandro Amenábar, Álex de la Iglesia, Fernando Trueba, Icíar Bollaín, Bigas Luna, and Carlos Saura. Some of them have also directed films starring world-famous actors.

SPORTS

If there is something that can unite Spanish people, it is sport. Being familiar with the main teams and players could help you socialize.

As in most European countries, soccer reigns. They love both playing it and watching it. Every town and village has its playing field, although only in the north do they have the luxury of grass (except for the professional stadiums). They also play basketball, tennis, golf, *pádel* (another type of tennis), and a whole range of other sports, including handball, which has goalposts as in soccer, but the ball is thrown, not kicked. In the Basque Country there are sports that exist nowhere else. These are similar to Scottish games, such as "tossing the caber"—throwing a large, heavy, wooden pole as far as you can—and involve great physical strength.

Soccer was introduced into Spain by the British in the second half of the nineteenth century and a professional league was set up in the 1920s. By

Soccer is Spain's most popular spectator sport. Here in action are teams Atlético de Madrid and UD Almería.

the 1950s it had surpassed bullfighting (which had been the most popular spectator sport since the eighteenth century) in popularity. Spain's leading clubs—Real Madrid, FC Barcelona, and Valencia Club FC—have a distinguished record in international competitions. The national selection, nicknamed La Furia (The Fury) or La Roja (The Red One in reference to the color of their first official kit), has also achieved great success. They won, for instance, the 2010 World Championship in South Africa. Atletico de Bilbao can brag of being the only team whose players are all local from el País Vasco.

At the end of the 1980s, soccer was challenged by basketball, whose popularity soared after Spain won the silver medal in the sport at the 1984 Olympics. There is a popular league, ACB (Basketball Clubs Association). The main teams are Real Madrid (who have won several European Leagues or Cups), Barcelona CF, Joventut, and Estudiantes. They all have international players.

More than thirty years ago the success of tennis stars Santana and Orantes made this game more popular. Later, Arantxa Sanchez Vicario, Conchita Martinez, Alex Corretja, and Sergi Bruguera were international players. Today, Rafael Nadal has won nineteen Grand Slams, and is regarded as one of the greatest players of all time, and there are public tennis courts all over the country.

There are also a lot of cycling clubs, especially in the northern regions. Federico Martín Bahamontes,

Champion road racing cyclist Alejandro Valverde.

Miguel Indurain, Abraham Olano, Pedro Delgado, and Óscar Freire are only a few Spain's past world champions. Now several other first-class professionals have taken their place, including Alberto Contador,

Abraham Olano, Alejandro Valverde, and Carlos Sastre. Although Spain is a very mountainous country and most cities do not have cycle lanes, nearly every teenager has a bicycle.

Other "big names" in sport are Alex Crevillé, Marc Marquez, and Dani Pedrosa (motorcycle racing); Mireia Belmonte (swimming); Carlos Sainz, Roberto Merhi, and Fernando Alonso (Formula One auto racing); Pol Amat and Santi Freixa (hockey); Javier Fernandez López (figure skating); and Ana María Izurieta (gymnastics).

Walking

The Spaniards are active users of their parks and countryside. Apart from the famous Camino de Santiago, there are walking routes all over Spain. *Excursionista* (hiker) clubs or groups of friends take to the mountains and nature reserves every weekend to enjoy the wonderful scenery. There is usually a meal at the end of it! On many mountain peaks you will see *hermitas*, small chapels dedicated to saints venerated in that area. It is worth braving the winding roads for the amazing views. At least once a year there will be a pilgrimage there that turns into a kind of town picnic, with communal *paella* or shared lunches. Some *hermitas* have a bar or restaurant attached.

As a nation, Spain does not have a good record for protecting its natural resources. Every summer there are numerous forest fires, many produced by high temperatures and lack of maintenance, and some by arsonists. Spain has the worst record in the EC for violating environmental protection rules.

LOTTERY AND GAMBLING

The Spanish are a nation of gamblers. Perhaps this is because they love excitement and taking risks, inherent in Spain in everything from bullfighting to driving, or perhaps it is simply the hope of making easy money. Whatever it is, there are more types of lottery, and bigger prizes to be won, in Spain than in any other country.

The oldest lottery, La Lotería Nacional, has been running since 1812. It earns half its money from the two Christmas lotteries: El Gordo (the fat one), just before Christmas, and El Niño (the child) on January 5, the day before *los reyes magos* (the Three Kings/Magi) bring the presents. These carry the biggest prizes, and in 1991 it was estimated that their takings (US $1,542 million, or £867 million) represented an average outlay of US $50 (£28) per Spanish adult. Almost everyone takes part, and many wait in line for hours to get their tickets from the most reputable *puestos* (newsstands/kiosks). The winning numbers are sung out on national television in a kind of Gregorian chant for several hours. Wherever you go on December 23 you will hear it.

There are other national lotteries, and also regional ones. The ONCE kiosks can be seen all over

Spain. They are owned by the Organización Nacional de Ciegos Españoles (National Organization for the Blind). This was created by Franco's government in 1938 to provide employment for the blind, and was exempt from tax. The blind sellers would stand on street corners with their tickets. By 1950 ONCE was able to provide a welfare system for its members, and new management meant it became more streamlined and successful. Today it is a great financial empire.

Apart from the lotteries, a vast amount of money is spent on slot machines (*máquinas tragaperras*), which can be heard bleeping away in the corner of every Spanish bar. In 1991 their net takings dwarfed that of the lottery (over US $2 billion, or £1.5 billion). Bingo also is enthusiastically played in Spain, but it is very strictly controlled, and played only in casinos, where you have to produce ID before being admitted.

CHAPTER SEVEN

TRAVEL, HEALTH, & SAFETY

FLYING

Spain has a number of international airports operated by AENA (the Spanish Airports and Air Navigation). Apart from the major airports of Madrid (Barajas) and Barcelona (El Prat), there are smaller ones serving the tourist resorts along the Mediterranean coast, such as the Elche–Alicante airport (in the Costa Blanca), and those of the Balear and Canary Islands. The national airline, Iberia (and its subsidiaries Vueling and Air Nostrum), operates a network of internal flights. The *puente aéreo* (air bridge) that links Madrid and Barcelona is the most important internal route, although in recent years it has started to be overtaken by high-speed railways. Barajas handles over twenty-seven million passengers a year; El Prat more than thirty-seven million.

DRIVING

Spaniards drive quickly and aggressively, and have little patience. You need to be constantly alert, and use your mirrors and indicators all the time. You are expected to show confidence and know where you are going; people will sound their horns or signal if you hesitate for even a moment.

Buy a good map or a GPS and try to work out your route before leaving home. In some areas towns will have their names in the local language. This can be confusing in the Basque Country, for example, where San Sebastian becomes Donostia and Vitoria is Gasteiz.

Legal Requirements

When driving in Spain you must carry with you your passport, or some other form of ID, your current driver's license, valid insurance papers, and the vehicle registration document. You should also have two red warning triangles, a reflective vest, a first-aid kit, a fire extinguisher, and a set of spare bulbs. For emergencies, many Spaniards also carry a blanket and antifreeze in winter.

The use of seat belts by all vehicle passengers is compulsory.

The police are more vigilant than they used to be about violations of traffic laws, and on-the-spot fines are compulsory for non-residents. Other fines are calculated according to the severity of the offense and the opinion of the police officer.

Mind the speed radars. Until 2015 they used to be hidden to catch drivers by surprise, but now it is possible to check their exact location. Yet, there are many mobile police controls at key points and on special days.

The legal drink driving limit is 0.05 percent (0.5 grams per liter of blood and 0.25 milligrams per liter of air), and Breathalyzer tests are frequent all over Spain. Make sure you are aware of speed restrictions—there are many speed traps.

It is illegal to use a cell phone while driving, although you can pull over to the side of the road for an emergency call or dial hands free. Motorists are required to use a hands-free kit, without earphone connections, fitted to the power supply of the car. Those who break the law face fines of up to 300 euros (around US $300).

The Roads
There are all types of roads, from fast modern highways to narrow country lanes. They are:

Autopistas, A or E (expressways). These are often toll roads. Speed limit, 75 mph (120 kmph).

Autovias (divided highways, or dual carriageways). These sometimes have only a central barrier, sometimes a wider safety zone. The speed limit is 62 mph (100 kmph).

Carreteras Nacionales, N or CN (main roads). Speed limit, 62 mph (100 kmph) where there is a hard shoulder and 56 mph (90 kmph) where there is none.

Carreteras Comarcales, C (country roads). Speed limit, 56 mph (90 kmph).

Carreteras Locales (byroads). Speed limit, 56 mph (90 kmph).

The speed limit in towns is 31 mph (50 kmph).

Toll Roads

These are first-rate, and have service stations approximately every 25 miles (40 km). The tolls are expensive, and are usually calculated according to distance traveled. You pay as you leave the toll road, but sometimes you receive a ticket when you enter that is to be handed in when you leave, to calculate what you owe. As you approach the *peaje* (toll booth), you will be confronted with several lanes. The *Telepago* lane is for cars that are fitted with a special chip on the windshield. The *Automatico* lane is for paying by credit card or the exact change. The *Manual* has an attendant who collects your fee. The lanes to use will display a green arrow (don't use one showing a red cross).

Parking

As a general rule, you may not park where the sidewalk is painted yellow, or, obviously, where a "no parking" sign is displayed. In major cities it is difficult to find free parking. There are parking spaces marked in blue, green, and orange where you can usually leave the car for up to two hours, and will have to purchase a ticket from a machine or an attendant. Where

RULES OF THE ROAD

- Drive on the right. Give way to traffic from the right, especially at traffic circles.
- Do not turn left if there is a solid line along the middle of the road. This is a major cause of accidents on fast roads. There will be a special lane on the right, signed *Cambio de sentido*, which will take you on to a side road, and will then cross back over the main road.
- Traffic lights are not always located on the streets. They are sometimes suspended high in the air above the traffic, and can be hard to see in the sun. If you sit at a green light for more than a second, expect hooting from behind you.
- Watch out on pedestrian crossings—especially if you are the pedestrian—as they do not give you the right of way. Always be very careful before stepping out. Cars may not always slow down.
- Flashing headlights can mean anything from "the police are ahead" (if coming toward you) to "get out of my way, you're driving too slowly" (from behind) or "you forgot to switch on the lights." Like the horn, they are overused.
- In keeping with their temperament, the Spanish often bend the rules a little. Don't be surprised when turn signals are ignored or people stop wherever they wish, and speed limits are ignored. Do not follow suit.

possible, look for underground parking with security. It can be worth paying more.

You will note, however, that the Spanish often pull in wherever they like, even stopping on crossings and sidewalks. Do not follow suit.

Penalties for parking infringements vary from town to town. If you park illegally, especially in a foreign car, you will almost certainly become a victim of the *grúa*, the local tow truck. Getting your car back is a hassle, and very expensive.

TRAINS

Mainline Trains

RENFE (Red Nacional de Ferrocarriles Españoles), the national network of Spanish railways, runs most of the nearly 9,500 miles (approx. 15,000 km) of railway in Spain, with fares that are among the cheapest in Europe. However, many of the trains are slow and uncomfortable, and do not have air-conditioning.

For medium and long distance journeys, the Intercity (IC), Euromed, Alvia, or TALGO are good options. They are fast, comfortable, and efficient. However, when choosing TALGO, you might be unlucky and get an old-fashioned train that can be quite uncomfortable. These trains will always have a "cafetería" (a small café/bar) on board, although the quality is indifferent and prices are high.

AVE (Alta Velocidad España, "Spanish High Velocity") covers medium and long distance routes connecting Madrid with Seville, Málaga, Barcelona, Valencia, Alicante, Huesca, and Gerona. You can now get from Madrid to Málaga in just over two hours instead of seven, depending on the number of stops.

The better the train, the more expensive the ticket. Check the various options available as there are discounts for frequent travelers and students. There are information desks at all the big stations. You can also book seats with authorized travel agents, who will charge a small commission but will usually be more helpful and relaxed. Always book a seat on long journeys.

AVE, Spain's high-speed rail network, with almost 2,000 miles (3,100 km) of track, connects the country's major cities.

Narrow-Gauge Trains

There are other railway companies in Spain in charge of the narrow-gauge tracks that still serve parts of the country, especially in the north. Some of the trains are used only by tourists, while others are a normal way of local travel. One example is FEVE (Ferrocarril de Vía Estrecha, the narrow-gauge line) running from Alicante to Denia on the Costa Blanca. Built in 1914 to transport fresh produce to Alicante, the 57-mile (93-km) route passes colorful fishermen's houses, deep gorges, and the whitewashed village of Altea.

Other tourist options are available. Some steam trains have been restored and brought back into use. One is the Tren de la Fresa (Strawberry Train) running from Madrid to the palace at Aranjuez, so called because the line was used to take fresh strawberries to the capital. The tradition is carried on to this day, with fresh strawberries being handed out to passengers.

If you want to experience the ultimate train journey, take one of the country's luxurious specials, built in the 1920s. The Transcantabrico follows the north coast of Spain from San Sebastian to Santiago de Compostela on an eight-day trip. The four coaches include a bar with disk jockey. At night the train parks in stations to allow passengers to get a good night's sleep.

In the south the Al Andalus Express is a mobile hotel consisting of twelve coaches, which follows a route taking in all the Moorish sites of Andalusia. There are two luxury restaurants, a bar, a lounge, and a games car.

There are many other interesting tourist routes to take in by train. See page 194 for more information.

INTERCITY BUSES

Throughout Spain there are many good private companies with coaches that are well maintained and offer cheap travel. They often take a more direct route than the trains and some offer an "express" service, which does not mean that the bus is faster, but it will be more comfortable. Most towns will have a bus terminal (*estación de autobús*). You can buy tickets here, from a travel agent, or online, and sometimes directly from the bus driver. It is recommended, however, to book in advance, especially for weekends and holidays. Long journeys will usually have short refreshment stops, but be sure to get back to the bus punctually. They may not wait for latecomers.

URBAN TRANSPORTATION

Many of Spain's cities have extensive bus, metro, and local train networks. The metro is the fastest and most efficient way of getting around. Valencia, however, has an efficient bus service and as it is a relatively small city it takes at most forty-five minutes to travel across it.

Most large cities have a metro system, identified by a red and white diamond shape marked "Metro" with station name below.

Metro (Underground Train Systems)

Madrid has thirteen underground lines, identified by a number and color-coded on maps. The service operates from 6:00 a.m. to 1:30 a.m. Tickets can be bought at all stations, from machines or staffed ticket booths. For multiple journeys buy a Metrobus ticket, valid for ten trips on the Metro or buses.

The service in Barcelona is open from 5:00 a.m. to midnight on Sunday to Thursday, and from 5:00 a.m. to 2:00 a.m. on Friday, Saturday, and on the eve of local holidays. There are tickets for single or multiple journeys. Tourist options include three-day and five-day tickets with unlimited journeys, or the airbus+bus+metro ticket that allows you to use the various types of transportation for unlimited travel and includes a return ticket to the airport. Check at the information desks for the available options.

Buses

Buses run daily from 6:30 a.m. to 11:30 p.m., and about every ten to fifteen minutes on most routes. Most bus stops have an electronic board displaying how long you have to wait for the buses to arrive.

There is also a night bus service after midnight called the Buho (owl) in Madrid and the Nitbus (nightbus) in Barcelona. Fewer buses run on Sundays and public holidays.

Bus stops have useful maps of the routes. Raise your arm to stop the bus. There is one standard fare for all journeys. The ticket can be bought once you are on the bus (many of the city buses only accept the correct change), or you can buy a Metrobus ticket, valid for ten trips by bus or metro. These can also be purchased from bus information stands, *estancos* (tobacconists), and newsstands.

Web Sites and Applications for Smartphones

Some useful Web sites on the subject of transportation appear on pages 194–95. Many Spanish cities offer apps for cell phones for all public transportation, with maps of bus routes and trainlines.

Taxis

There is no shortage of taxis in Spain, and they are quite affordable in comparison with other European countries. They are different colors in different cities (white in Madrid and Valencia; black and yellow in Barcelona), but all have a sign on the roof with a green light that comes on when the cab is available. There are taxi stands, or you can just stop one in the street. In Barcelona there is also a private taxi company driven by, and exclusively for, women, easily recognized by the color of their cars—pink. They have meters, but there is an extra charge at night, on weekends, and if you have luggage. If you take a cab at an airport or train station, or this is your destination, there is an initial fixed fare of about 5 or 6 euros. If you are going on a long journey, ask and agree on the approximate price beforehand. As for tipping, people usually give 10 percent, or just round up the fare.

WHERE TO STAY

Tourism has brought a great deal of wealth to Spain, but it has also spoiled the Mediterranean coastline, where high-rise hotels and apartment complexes were thrown up without much thought for overall design in the 1960s and 1970s. There is no shortage of accommodation generally, either in these coastal resorts or inland. All large towns and cities have plenty of places to stay, ranging from luxurious hotels to cheap and cheerful *hostales*. Local tourist offices have lists of what is available. It is always worth making reservations in advance, especially if you are visiting a town during festival time.

Hotels

Hotels in Spain conform to European standards, and range from five stars down, according to the facilities offered. You can be sure you will enjoy the facilities and services promised. They come in all shapes and sizes; some are traditional, others completely modern.

One type of hotel peculiar to Spain is the *parador*. These started as a group of historic buildings converted into hotels by the government in the 1920s, in part to preserve them, but also to encourage travel to less-visited parts of the country. Today, there are eighty-five such establishments spread throughout Spain. About a third of them are historic buildings, while others are tastefully designed new buildings constructed in styles authentic to their regions, often in picturesque villages or highly scenic locations. The older buildings have all been restored, and all have modern hotel facilities.

Hostales

These abound in all cities, and tourist offices will give you a list. They are cheaper than hotels and also have a "star" rating. They are often housed on two floors of an apartment complex, with a reception area, television room, dining room, and some bedrooms on one floor, and the remainder of the bedrooms on the floor above. *Hostales* are usually family-run, and the staff may speak only Spanish. Bedrooms will not always have their own bathrooms, and meals are not usually included. A simple breakfast may be available.

Albergues

These are youth hostels and other types of basic lodgings. They have dormitory-style rooms and a dining room and kitchen where you can cook for yourself. They are usually situated near major railway stations in the cities, or in some of the nature reserves scattered throughout Spain. They are cheap, basic, and populated mainly by young backpackers.

Apartamentos

Self-contained apartments for rent in the coastal regions, these can be anything from rooms furnished with the basics to small *villas* with a garden area. Prices will depend on size, location, and the time of year. (Apartments for long-term residency are called *pisos.*)

Another form of accommodation that has become popular is renting a room in a private home with shared facilities. This is often a more affordable option. You will generally have access to common facilities such as the living room, kitchen, and bathroom, and will be provided with towels, sheets and a few toiletries. Some "landlords" are very hospitable and offer tourist information, tips and even breakfast just like bed and breakfasts do. See page 195 for more information about this service.

Agroturismo

This is a new trend that is very popular in the rural areas. Large houses in the country rent out rooms in an attempt to open up rural areas to tourism, for both locals and foreigners. *Agroturismo* can also be found in traditional tourist destinations famous for their sea and sun. Mallorca is a clear example of this diversification.

HEALTH AND INSURANCE

In Spain you will always need to visit a pharmacy to buy prescription drugs, and even those that are available without a prescription. Pharmacists also deal with minor health problems and can provide some medications that in other countries would require a prescription, such as antibiotics.

There is a very good public health system that works alongside an excellent private sector. Generally, hospitals are of a very high standard and nurses, doctors, and surgeons enjoy a high-level of respect nationally and internationally. This has positioned Spain as one of the favori7te "health and medical destinations" for other Europeans. Some European patients come to Spain during their vacation to receive free or very affordable treatments and surgery that in their home country would be much more expensive. This phenomenon and its accompanying financial loss is often a subject of national debate.

Private travel insurance for all visitors is highly recommended.

COVID-19
Spain was among the countries most severely hit by the Covid pandemic in 2020, which affected the tourism sector particularly badly. The government's public safety measures, however, elicited a boom of social and cultural initiatives, and created a remarkable sense of social solidarity across the land.

CHAPTER EIGHT

BUSINESS BRIEFING

People coming to Spain to do business are often struck by three things: the cultural differences between the regions, the need for a continuing relationship to ensure its success, and the fact that the Spaniards are prone to improvising or making last-minute changes to plans.

Spain's most important business hubs are in Madrid and Barcelona and their surrounding areas, and in Andalusia in the south. The Catalans' approach to business and work is different from that of people in the other regions of Spain. They can come across as direct, even abrupt, and not as expressive as one might have expected. Other Spaniards consider them hardworking, frugal, aloof, and humorless. The Catalans find the *Madrileños*, the people from Madrid, arrogant, bureaucratic, and extravagant tricksters who like showing off. The Andalusians tend to be more laid-back, more prone to long lunch breaks and to doing business outside the office. Despite these stereotypes, however, attitudes to time, appointments, and deadlines are often an individual matter.

What is common to all, however, is the fact that, as in Italy and Portugal, good personal relations are the *sine qua non* of successful business. With good personal relations, a business may still fail, but without them there will be no business at all. Spanish business people have always networked, even before this activity became fashionable. Deadlines may not be adhered to unless contact is maintained. The personal relationship gives importance to the matter at hand, and deliveries will be ready if you follow them up.

COMPANY ORGANIZATION AND BEHAVIOR

Spain has two forms of company, the stock company, Sociedad Anónima (SA), and the limited company, Sociedad de Responsibilidad Limitada (SRL). Companies with more than fifty employees must have a works committee. Companies with more than five hundred employees have an employee representative on the board. The number of *autónomos* or *trabajadores por cuenta propia* (freelancers or self-employed) has multiplied in recent years as a result of high unemployment rates. The government has tried to make it easier for start-up companies; however, in comparison with countries such as the Netherlands, there is still much to be done to improve areas of the bureaucracy and taxes.

Offices tend to work a forty-hour week, from
9:00 a.m. to 1:00 or 2:00 p.m., with two hours for lunch,
and then from 3:00 or 4:00 p.m. to 6:00 or 7:00 p.m. or
even later. These hours may be adjusted in the south to
allow for a longer lunch break and to avoid the main
heat of the day. Deals are often agreed upon in principle
over lunch, dinner, or a coffee, with subordinates
fleshing out the details with you later, in the office.

People are sometimes allowed to take a four-day
weekend over public holidays. In July and August, most
people go away on vacation and, depending on their
industry, offices may change their working hours, have
only a skeleton staff, or often, close down altogether for
a month. The legal amount of holidays is 2.5 days per
month worked, which amounts to 30 days annually.

Leadership and Hierarchy

Traditionally the Spanish management style has
been "top down," with all key decisions being made
by the boss. This is typical of the older established
companies and family firms, where the president is
the absolute controller and subordinate positions are
held by members of the family. Knowledge of English
is not automatic among older managers, who may
speak French as their first business language. However,
such working practices are radically changing. Today
new employees need to know more than two or
three languages, but it will take several more years
until companies are able to conduct their business
completely bilingually. Depending on the company you

are dealing with, you may need to find an interpreter or check whether there is a younger manager on the staff who can serve as interpreter. Spain does have a professionally trained cadre of managers, many of whom have studied internationally and are up-to-date on modern management techniques, and speak excellent English.

A Spanish boss (*jefe*) is expected to make decisions and to be courageous. He (or she, though it usually is a he) is also expected to work at gaining and maintaining the personal loyalty of his subordinates. His decisions will be concise, concrete, and short-term, with clear instructions as to how to implement them. However, managers may not feel committed to implementing them, and will pass even small decisions back up the line. This is especially true in the civil service, where immense bureaucracy can slow things down. In many older companies, written objectives and profiles are unusual, as are appraisals.

Spanish managers tend to work less from logic than from intuition, and they pride themselves on their personal influence with their staff. A Spanish manager is expected to be aware not only of the business lives but also of the personal lives of their staff and the people they are doing business with, and to be prepared to deal with problems in either area. Instructions are never given coldly. Warmth is an important part of giving orders and instructions, especially in the south, but the underlying authority is always clear. Logic is often secondary to force of emotion.

Human Responsiveness

If a Spanish employee approaches his or her boss with a personal problem, it is important to pay attention to it immediately, even if only to make an appointment to deal with it or discuss it in more detail later. The personal and human dimension takes priority.

The Spanish executive generally likes to work near his or her family. A few years may be spent studying and working in Madrid, but then employment is usually sought in the hometown. In many companies connections (colloquially *enchufe*), rather than qualifications or aptitude, are still the key to recruitment. Education is still regarded as extremely important, but other qualities such as professional and international experience as well as proactivity and responsiveness are expected as part of the package. The qualifications for promotion are personal loyalty, friendship, and ability, usually in that order. Intelligence alone may seem a bit suspect. These values together with the high rate of unemployment have created immense frustration among people of all ages. And many of them have chosen to leave the country in an attempt to find better opportunities elsewhere. Sometimes they do, sometimes they are not so lucky. Overall, however, the country has suffered a major brain drain since 2008.

BUSINESS STYLE

Although Spain is a hot country, appearance is important, and people are expected to dress in an acceptably businesslike, formal and stylish fashion—dark suits or navy blue blazers and ties for men, and formal suits or dresses, always with nylons, for women. Jackets and ties may be removed in the office, especially in summer. Symbols of wealth in clothes, watches, cars, and jewelry are usually a good sign; they show that you have done well. The Spaniards take great pride in their possessions, and set store by quality and taste. Your Mont Blanc pen or Cartier watch will be quietly noticed and appreciated, but not commented upon.

Spanish business style is generally quite informal and relaxed, but first meetings are formal. A senior man, for example the president of a company, named Don Sr. José Antonio López, might be addressed as Don José Antonio or Don José. Use the formal *usted* (abb. *Ud.*), and change to the informal *tú* only if suggested by your hosts. You will probably move to first-name terms rapidly, and continue in this informal style thereafter. If this happens, do not be surprised if e-mails start ending with "*Estamos en contacto*" ("Let's keep in touch") or even "*Un abrazo*."

It is important to have a relationship based on trust. It is also important not to be overassertive, as this may impinge on personal pride. The Spaniards take more pride in their personal qualities, in particular personal honor, than in their business or technical excellence. The personal touch is all-important, and getting out of the office to chat and "network" is part of the job. That is the way many businesses work. One cup of coffee with you may count for more than a hundred exchanges of e-mails. In a highly competitive atmosphere where most of the population is often over educated, this is a way of standing out. If you are in another country, then a telephone or videoconference conversation can fulfill the same function.

Lunchtime at work often happens. Even if it is just an hour, people will mix with their colleagues in a café to have "*el menú del día*" or in the company's kitchen or lunchroom for the staff. However, the bosses do not mix with the staff and tend to have lunch separately at a restaurant where they are well known.

WOMEN IN BUSINESS

Despite the traditional Spanish *macho* image, there are many women in middle and senior management

Women tend to occupy middle and senior positions in a company but rarely enjoy the top roles.

positions, and their qualifications ensure that they are universally accepted. That said, however, you will not meet many women at the top of a Spanish company—unless she is the daughter or granddaughter of the founder. Businesswomen expect a completely professional attitude from the men they are dealing with in business. A lunch or dinner invitation will be considered as part of the business relationship.

THE BUSINESS RELATIONSHIP

To do business in Spain you must first earn the trust of your Spanish counterpart by establishing a personal rapport. Your business partners will be hospitable, and any social invitation should be regarded as an investment in a trusting relationship. Talking about families and children is an important part of this, and having photos of your family ready to show will help greatly in building the relationship. It will demonstrate to your Spanish counterpart that you have roots in your society, and therefore a stake in ensuring that things are done correctly. At job interviews you might be asked about your parents' profession, your family members, or personal status. Companies like to know their staff. Contrary to other cultures, CVs are expected to have a professional ID photo.

The social relationship extends to small family favors. If you can help a relative or friend of your business partner in some way, it will be seen as a real favor, and will be of immense value in building trust. A successful business relationship has to move beyond mere good business relations.

For a man in business, pride and the *macho* image are still important. Crucial to Spanish business is the concept of honor and of not losing dignity. Spanish business partners are men and women of their word. Once you have established a relationship, they will not let you down. By the same token, you must be careful not to do anything that lets them down in the eyes of their peers.

One key aspect of this is the employment of Spanish agents to act on your behalf. They are your eyes and ears in the market, and once you employ them you must work with them—they will be very unhappy if you make any move behind their back. Make sure you choose such contacts wisely, as they can make or break your presence in the Spanish market.

FLEXIBILITY

A Spanish businessperson, although equipped with agendas and timetables, also prides him or herself on being flexible. This often means three things: that planning may seem more haphazard; projects may progress at a slower rate than you would expect or like; and that they are open to new ideas and changes if these are interesting and reasonable. Spaniards know how to cram a lot in. This means that they are essentially multitasking, prioritizing continuously, juggling a number of things, and reacting to the most important or urgent requirement.

The Spaniards prefer long-term visions and short-term plans. They can do this because of the immense importance of networking in Spanish society. It has been maintained that they can achieve in three days what for an American or German might take three months, because they can do it all personally, on the telephone. Their years of networking mean that they can achieve things through personal contact that would be quite difficult for their counterparts in Europe or the US. One of the most valuable possessions at work for a Spanish businessperson is their address book, with contacts for their clients, suppliers, business people, and other key persons.

MAKING APPOINTMENTS

The Spaniards, like the British, write the day first, then the month, then the year, so November 15, 2020 is written 15.11.20. When making an appointment, book ahead, and then telephone and confirm it before arrival. When you arrive for an appointment, the most appropriate way to announce yourself is to state your name and position or company when presenting your business card to the receptionist, who will let your Spanish contact know that you have arrived. You should be punctual, though sometimes you might be kept waiting between ten and thirty minutes. However, Spanish businesspeople are more and more international and they have got used to different business practices.

Keep in mind the normal business working hours, and remember that hours are often reduced or offices closed in general holiday periods. Avoid scheduling appointments around Easter, Christmas, or in August.

COMMUNICATION STYLE

The Spanish business communication style is relaxed and friendly, and relies above all on the human touch. It is important when sending a business e-mail to a Spaniard to be slightly more long-winded and warmer than you might be in a similar e-mail to an American or British contact. Use greetings such as *Estimado/a* (Dear)— avoid *Querido/a* which has a more personal meaning—to begin your communication, and *Saludos*, or *Saludos cordiales* or *Atentamente* (similar to Regards or Best regards) to close with. When the relationship becomes closer or more personal your first line can also be "*Buenos días Miguel*," ("Good morning Miguel,") and when it is a follow-up you can simply use the name followed by a comma. On the telephone, too, do not forget the human side.

MEETINGS

In Spain, the function of a meeting can be to get to know clients, to communicate instructions, to give an update on a project or topic, or to deal with an urgent issue. Meetings usually have a scheduled agenda, although very often new topics come up that can extend the proceedings. Depending on their relevance, they will be addressed immediately, left until the end, or scheduled for another meeting. The final decision will always remain with the boss, and if he or she cannot take part in the full discussion they will usually check in to make their presence known in the course of the meeting.

The Spanish will usually begin a meeting with a long speech that serves to establish their own status and qualifications as well as to outline their aims. This is followed by an equally long response from the other side. It is important during a meeting to find points of agreement to comment on wherever possible. Honor demands that a Spanish boss should not be contradicted in public, and a "compliant" foreigner may well gain concessions in a more relaxed atmosphere over lunch or dinner.

The meetings culture is not well established in all companies, and the idea of thrashing things out to arrive at a common agreement is not universally recognized, nor are action points or follow-ups. It is important for the person in the chair, however, to win everyone over to his or her point of view. The chairperson will either make the decisions or will have to put the decision made to the boss for ratification.

Spanish managers are quite individualistic, and will use a meeting to score personal points. They have an expressive style and negotiations can be loud, with frequent interruptions, and people called in at short notice to contribute to the negotiation. It is important not to be upset by conversational overlap, which is not felt to be rude in Spain. Everybody prepares the basics, but negotiations (often lengthy) depend on intuition and thinking on your feet rather than the careful preparation of, say, German and Swiss companies. The personal touch is enhanced by strong eye contact. Spaniards want to be able to "read your eyes," to know who you are.

PRESENTATIONS

Spaniards are often more concerned about giving a good impression and are not always the most dedicated listeners. They may appear to be less interested in the content and more in your style and appearance. They will observe your physical characteristics, your mannerisms, and your attitude and willingness to participate in the congenial socializing that will follow. If you are making a "substance" presentation, keep it short, and use a few imaginative phrases that people will remember. The Spaniards do not appreciate *palabrería* (empty verbosity) in business meetings or negotiations. They will want to interject and discuss points, so limit your presentation to thirty minutes.

PLANNING AND CONTROL

The dependence on the personal relationship means
that standard company functions, such as strategic
planning, and even financial business plans, may be
based on business sense and intuition rather than on
systematic data. Schedules, budgets, and forecasts
will be rough guides only. Everything must be done
by personal negotiation, although written proof such
as contracts or e-mails are requested. If they have not
called you to confirm a delivery, it is recommended
that you get in touch with them and find out whether
the stock has been delivered or even left the warehouse.
"Inspect, not expect," should be your motto.

BUSINESS ENTERTAINING

Be prepared to spend some time outside the office on
building and maintaining good relations. Although
today's business world no longer always allows for a
siesta in the afternoon—despite being world famous,
nowadays it mostly happens during weekends—the
Spaniards still start work early and finish late, going
out to dinner as late as 10:00 p.m. and finishing at
2:00 a.m. Weekend socializing can go on far later. Be
prepared for the strain on your constitution—and on
your digestion!

Business entertaining usually takes place in
restaurants. If you are invited to a Spanish home, it

may just be for a drink before moving on to dinner in a restaurant. You may otherwise be taken first for *tapas* in a café or bar.

Traditionally Spanish business protocol dictates that you wait until coffee is served at the end of the meal before bringing up the subject of business. However, as companies adopt international business practices and get busier they like to make the most of every second they have in their meetings.

THE PERSONAL TOUCH

A Spanish representative, working in Spain for a London-based British company, had for some months been underperforming in the market. An executive of the British company flew over to visit the offices in an attempt to find out what had gone wrong. He talked to each staff member personally, then took them all out to lunch, and generally formed a good relationship with them. "Now that we feel we know you," said some of the staff, as he left, "we'll try to do better for your products." And they did. Sales rose 50 percent.

Remember that whoever has extended the invitation pays the bill. If you have been invited out for a meal, you should return the compliment at a later date, but when doing so you should be careful not to mention "repaying" your hosts. When the time comes to choose a restaurant, ensure that it is an excellent one, as the Spaniards are extremely appreciative of fine food and wine, and will respect you for your good taste! Do not forget that many restaurants close for a month of vacation or open only during the evening or weekends, especially some of the more superior ones.

GIFT GIVING

Gifts are not usually given at a first meeting, but may serve as a sign of willingness to establish the relationship at a later date. They may also be given at the conclusion of successful negotiations. If you receive a gift, you should open it immediately. A stylish ballpoint pen, a small case of local wine, or produce are typical gifts.

If you are taking gifts, do not give anything too extravagant, or your generosity may be perceived as a bribe. Presents of single malt whiskey, quality English gin, or chocolates are very acceptable. If you want to give a bottle of Spanish wine, make sure that it is a special one, such as Vega Sicilia. Your country's local crafts and illustrated books related to your home region are also often appreciated. Only give a gift advertising your company name if it is discreet and tasteful.

On the rare occasion that you might be invited for a meal at a Spanish home, take a box of good chocolates, or dessert items such as attractive little pastries, or flowers—but count these, for thirteen flowers are always considered bad luck. Be sure to avoid buying dahlias or chrysanthemums, as these flowers are associated with death.

THE BOTTOM LINE

In business, as in most areas of Spanish life, the importance of personal relationships must not be underestimated. At first there is formality, but once introductions are over a more personal, informal approach is expected. However, dignity must always be maintained, and respect and honor are necessary for building trust and a working relationship.

Spanish business is "multitasking"—many things are dealt with at the same time, not separately. You, too, will be expected to be flexible. You should prioritize tasks and develop a good working relationship with both colleagues and subordinates. Good contacts are crucial as the concept of *enchufe* (the right contact) is a part of business life. If you are well considered by the right people, you are on your way toward success. Your product will be more easily accepted once your business partners accept you and like you.

But management practices are changing in Spain. The new and professionally trained managers have adopted a more decentralized, team-based, target-oriented, and quality-focused management.

CHAPTER NINE

COMMUNICATING

LANGUAGE

Spanish is the official language of Spain and of many other countries: Argentina, Bolivia, Chile, Colombia, Costa Rica, Cuba, the Dominican Republic, Ecuador, El Salvador, Equatorial Guinea, Guatemala, Honduras, Mexico, Nicaragua, Panama, Paraguay, Peru, Uruguay, and Venezuela. It is also the official language of the commonwealth of Puerto Rico, and is widely spoken in several other nations, including the United States of America, Morocco, and the Philippines.

Spanish and English vie for the position of the world's second most-spoken language after Chinese. In 1999, Spanish had 332 million speakers, while English had 322 million. Today 470 million people claim Spanish as their mother tongue. The rise has been such that in 2050 the Spanish-speaking community of the US is expected to be the largest in the world.

Castilian (Castellano)

Although generally known as Spanish, the correct name for Spain's official language is Castilian. It began as a dialect spoken in northern Spain, but became the language of the court of the kingdom of Castile and León in the twelfth century. When Isabella and Ferdinand united their kingdoms of Castile and Aragon, it became the official language of the state. Like other European languages it stems from Latin, but has also adopted words from other languages, including many Arabic words from the time of Moorish dominance.

There are differences in accent and, to a lesser extent, in vocabulary, in Castilian in various regions of the country. The most significant difference is in the pronunciation of the letter combinations "ce," "ze," and "za." In northern Castile, where the language is said to be spoken in its purest form, this is pronounced as a soft English "th;" in southern and western Spain it is pronounced as an English "s." The "s" pronunciation is also found in Latin American Spanish. There is no snobbery about accents in Spanish. Your accent tells the listener which area you come from, not which class you belong to.

Castilian is the country's most widely spoken language, although nearly 30 percent of the population have a different first language. These languages include Catalan (12 percent of the population), Galician (8 percent), and Basque (just over 1 percent). The constitution of 1978 gave the dominant regional languages and dialects official status, along with Castilian. Those stipulated are Catalan in Catalonia and in the Balearic Islands; Valencian in Valencia; *Euskera* (Basque) in the Basque Country and in the territory of Navarre; Aragonese in Aragon; and *Gallego* (Galician) in Galicia. Asturian and Aranese, spoken in the Aran Valley (Catalonia) are other languages that are protected, although they do not have co-official status. All of these languages except *Euskera* (Basque) are Romance languages that evolved from Latin. *Euskera* is a "language isolate," totally unrelated to any other language. Many of these languages are taught regularly in school and used in radio and television broadcasts within their regions.

Spain's tradition of regionalism has been a major factor in recognizing the various languages. Other countries in Europe have several local languages, but few of these have official recognition. For the foreigner in Spain this will not cause any difficulties. Castilian is spoken and understood everywhere, although in some areas people will not be as fluent in it as in their local language. However, if you learn a few words of any local language people will appreciate your efforts.

Catalan

Catalan is closely related to Provençal, a language spoken in southern France, and is spoken by the majority of the population in Catalonia, Valencia, and the Balearic Islands. There are differences in the way Catalan is spoken in these three regions, and there are continuous politically motivated disputes as to whether Valencian is a Catalan dialect or a distinct language. It has a long and distinguished history as a literary language. It flourished especially during the Middle Ages but declined after the fifteenth century. A revival known as the *Renaixença* (Renaissance), which began in the mid-nineteenth century, renewed interest in the language leading to the Pompeu Fabra grammar, the basis of Catalan as it is taught today.

Galician (Gallego)

This is spoken in Galicia, in the northwestern corner of Spain, and is the ancestor of modern Portuguese. It was the language of courtly literature until the fourteenth century, when it was displaced by Castilian. From then until the late nineteenth century, when there was a literary revival, its use was limited to everyday speech, and it was more common among country people than in the cities. In neighboring Asturias, the ancient local language is still spoken.

Basque (Euskera)

This is the most distinctive of the languages spoken in Spain. Neither a Romance nor an Indo-European language, it predates the arrival of the Romans in Spain. Until the end of the nineteenth century

Basque was spoken mostly in the countryside, and it had no significant literary tradition. In the twentieth century, and especially since it was made the official language of the Basque Country (Euskadi) in 1978, it has been used in all forms of writing.

On page 189 are a few phrases in the various languages to get you started. You will notice that questions and exclamations in written forms are indicated by an inverted question mark (¿) or exclamation mark (¡) at the beginning of the sentence, and then a standard one at the end of the sentence. This avoids confusion between questions or exclamations and statements, which in speech may differ only in the tone of voice used, and this cannot be seen when written.

SPEAKING SPANISH

Spanish is considered one of the easiest foreign languages to learn, yet some foreigners live in Spain for years and never learn it or any of the other languages spoken here. Especially on the *costas* (coasts) there are foreign communities that are almost self-sufficient, and the local people involved with them often learn to speak the dominant language (usually English or German). However, if you have a basic knowledge of Spanish, and use it, this will show that you have an interest in the culture, and it will be greatly appreciated.

Spain is a great country for practicing the language. The basic grammar is straightforward, but in any case nobody worries if your Spanish is not grammatically correct, or if you make mistakes. In tourist areas the local people will probably be able to communicate in different languages, but away from there even stumbling Spanish will open up the possibility of communication. A gregarious people, the Spanish love talking, and will do their best to converse with you.

A phrase book translating basic phrases from your own language to Spanish and a pocket dictionary are probably all you need, to begin with. However, if you plan to stay for a while or will be visiting Spain often, consider doing a basic Spanish course. It will pay dividends.

Spanish Pronunciation
Written Spanish is almost completely phonetic. Once you know how to pronounce the letters and where to stress the words, you can make a good attempt at reading it. Here are the most basic rules:

The Spanish alphabet consists of twenty-eight letters: *a, b, c, ch, d, e, f, g, h, i, j, k, l, ll, m, n, ñ, o, p, q, r, s, t, u, v, x, y, z.*

The vowels, *a, e, i, o,*and *u* sound like the vowels in the English words "ha," "hay," "he," "ho," and "who."

The consonants *b* and *v* are pronounced very similarly to each other, as are *ll* and *y.* Spanish

SOME USEFUL PHRASES

ENGLISH	CASTILIAN	CATALAN	GALICIAN	BASQUE
Hello	Hola	Hola	Ola	Kaixo
Good morning	Buenos días	Bon dia	Bon dia	Egun on
Good afternoon	Buenas tardes	Bona tarda	Boa tarde	Arratsalde on
Good night	Buenas noches	Bona nit	Boa noite	Gabon
Good-bye	Adiós	Adéu	Adeus	Agur
Please	Por favor	Si us plau	Por favor	Mesedez
Thank you	Gracias	Gracies	Gracias	Eskerrik asko
Excuse me	Perdón	Perdona	Desculpa	Barkatu
Cheers!	¡Salud!	Salut!	Saude!	Topa!
Is there a hotel near here?	¿Hay un hotel por aquí?	Hi ha un hotel per aquí?	Hai algun hotel aquí perto?	Bal al da hotelik hemen inguruan?
Where is the bus station?	¿Donde está la estación de autobus?	On es l'estació d'autobus?	Onde está a estación de autobus?	Non dago autobus-geltokia?

speakers also drop *h* sounds at the beginning of words, so that *horario* (schedule) and *historia* (history) are pronounced as if they were spelled *orario* and *istoria*. These three elements of the language account for the most common mistakes made by people learning Spanish as a second language: confusing *b* with *v*, pronouncing *ll* as though in English, and sounding the *h* at the beginning of words where it should be silent.

Most Spanish words ending with a vowel or the consonants *n* or *s* are pronounced with the stress on the penultimate syllable, for example, *vino, casa, abuela, viven, antes* (pronounced *bee*no, *kass*a, ab*way*la, *bee*ben, *an*tes, and meaning wine, house, grandmother, they live, before).

Words ending in consonants other than *n* or *s,* however, are stressed on the last syllable, for example, *ciudad, feliz, municipal, hotel* (pronounced seeoo*dad*, fell*eeth*, moonithi*pal*, o*tel*, meaning city, happy, municipal, hotel). All words that are exceptions to these rules have an accent to show where the stress falls, for example, *estación, avión,* López (estathee*on*, meaning station, avi*on,* meaning airplane, and *Lo*peth, a surname).

FACE TO FACE

Whatever language you may be speaking, the Spanish have a typically Mediterranean manner. They stand quite close to the person they are speaking to, and will often touch the other person to emphasize a point. They gesticulate a lot, which can help the learner if the conversation is in Spanish, and they speak loudly. The combination of volume and forceful gestures often make it difficult to be sure whether two people are having a normal conversation or an argument! If you tell someone you do not understand them, they tend to repeat exactly the same sentence, maybe a little louder or slower, instead of trying to find a different way to say it—this is especially true for the older generations.

In a formal situation the voice may be slightly lowered, gestures will be restrained, and the "*usted*" form will be used. As we have seen, this is similar to the *vous* form in French, but it is not used as frequently. It is a polite and respectful form of address that is reserved for speaking to older people, or perhaps to business associates in a formal meeting.

There are no taboo subjects, but to start with it is probably safer to stay with topics of general interest rather than to ask somebody a lot of personal questions. Sports, the weather and especially complimentary remarks and questions about the local area will always get the conversation going, and you will soon find points of common interest to discuss. As mentioned before, if the Spanish are talking negatively about themselves and their culture, you should be diplomatic and not join in.

SERVICES

Mail

The post office (*Correos*) is open from 9:00 a.m. to 2:00 p.m. on weekdays, and until 1:00 p.m. on Saturday; you can buy stamps from a tobacconist (*estanco*).

The mail is delivered once a day, before 3:00 p.m. Small packages will be delivered to the house, but larger ones will be kept at the post office and will have to be collected.

Telephone

The national company, Telefónica, controls line rental, although it now has to compete with other companies over the prices of calls. You may use different companies for different types of call. Every Spanish province has a different two- or three-figure prefix. Telephone numbers consist of nine digits, including the prefix. The national code is 0034 or +34.

Telephone booths (*cabinas*) are not very common. However, there are plenty of "*locutorios*"—small businesses where you can access the Internet, call your country at cheaper rates, and get special cell phone deals. The standard Spanish answer when answering the phone is "*Digame*," or "*Diga*," meaning "Tell me," or "Tell," respectively.

Cell phones in Spain operate on the same principles as anywhere else in the world, although fees tend to be higher. And, naturally, young people keep in touch on smartphones and laptops via social media.

CONCLUSION

The Spanish are generally relaxed, sociable, and family-loving. With the outdoor life of sunshine, crowds of people, good food and drink, and gossip, activity, and good humored bustle everywhere, especially during weekends and in summer, you will probably quickly get into the swing of it all and start to love the Spanish way of life.

As a business traveler, you might see some of the Spanish traits from a different angle. Their flexibility and striking ability to change and reprioritize may seem chaotic, but in time you will understand their reasons. You are sure to find your Spanish contacts to be friendly and hospitable, and interested in you personally. Be sure to show them the same interest. Once they get to know you, you will be important to them, and your business is likely to flourish as a result.

Whatever your reason for going there, knowing more about the Spanish and their culture will help you to make the most of your time in Spain, and to have realistic expectations. Above all, it will help you to be at ease in a country where the individual is important and enjoying life is a priority.

¡Viva España!

APPENDIX: ONLINE RESOURCES

There are plenty of Web sites giving useful information about Spain, and it is a good idea to consult them before you go.

Tourism
www.tourspain.es/en-us Official Web site for the promotion of Spain abroad
www.tourspain.es Official Spanish National Tourist Office
www.spaindata.com General data on Spain
www.okspain.com Tourist information about all parts of Spain

General Information
www.spainexpat.com A Web page for expats living in Spain
www.viamichelin.com Detailed maps for all regions of Spain
www.idealspain.com Information on many sporting and leisure activities
www.marcaespana.es/en Official site of Brand Spain
www. extranjeros.empleo.gob.es Spanish Secretariat of Immigration and Emigration
www.112.es Emergency Services
www.policia.es National Police

History and Culture
www.spanishculture.com Official site for the promotion of Spanish culture

Transportation
www.ctm-madrid.es Madrid
www.tmb.net Barcelona
www.fgc.es FGC (Catalunya, Costa Daurada)
www.emtvalencia.es Valencia public urban bus network
www.fgv.es Valencian Community's Railways (Costa Blanca)
www.juntadeandalucia.es temas/transporte/publico
metropolitano.html Andalusian metropolitan transport information
www.tib.org/portal/en Mallorca (Balear Islands)
www.titsa.com Tenerife (Canary Islands)
www.euskotren.es Euskotren (Basque Country)
www.feve.es Feve (Northern Spain)
www.renfe.es National railways' site
www.moovitapp.com/espanol Transport information for smartphones

Airports
www.aena.es Spanish Airports and Air Navigation
www.iberia.es Iberia Flights
www.vueling.es Iberia's low cost airline

Special Tourist Train Routes
www.alandalusexpreso.com Al Andalus Express
www.ffe.es/delicias Tren de la Fresa ("Strawerry Train")
www.trendesoller.com Tren de Soller (Mallorca)
www.cremallerademontserrat.cat Montserrat (Catalunya)
www.renfe.com/trenesturisticos/eng Other routes: Cervantes Train, Medieval Train, Tren de Sigüenza, and El Expreso de La Robla.

Accommodation
www.paradores.es/en Spanish *paradores*
www.agroturismorural.com Agrotourism and rural tourism in Spain
www.airbnb.es Holiday rooms and apartments rental
www.wimdu.es Holiday rooms and apartments rental
www.reaj.com Spanish network of hostels
www.residencias.eu Spanish Dormitory Net

Studying in Spain
www.cervantesinstitute.es Cervantes Institute (Spanish culture and language)
www.rae.es Official Spanish Dictionary and Thesaurus
www.studyinspain.info Studying in Spain
www.universia.es Spanish higher education information

Health
www.sespas.es Spanish Society of Public Health and Sanitary Administration

Business
www.icex.es Spanish Institute for Foreign Trade

FURTHER READING

Carr, Raymond (ed.). *Spain: A History*. Oxford: Oxford University Press, 2000.

Catlos, Brian A. *Kingdoms of Faith: A New History of Islamic Spain*. New York: Basic Books, 2018.

Franco, Silvana. *Great Tapas*. New York: Lorenz Books, 2000.

Goodwin, Robert. *Spain: The Centre of the World 1512–1682*. London: Bloomsbury, 2016.

Goulding, Matt. *Grape, Olive, Pig: Deep Travels Through Spain's Food Culture*. New York: Harper Wave, 2016.

Howse, Christopher. *The Train in Spain: Ten Great Journeys throughout the Interior*. London: Bloomsbury, 2013.

_____ *A Pilgrim in Spain*. New York: Continuum Publishing Corporation, 2011.

Orti, Pilar with Paul Read. *The A to Z of Spanish Culture: A Condensed Look at Life in Spain*. Morrisville: Lulu Press, 2014.

Phillips, William D. and Carla Rahn Phillips. *A Concise History of Spain*. Cambridge: Cambridge University Press, 2016.

Tóibín, Colm. *Homage to Barcelona*. London: Simon and Schuster, 1990.

Tremlett, Giles. *Ghosts of Spain: Travels Through Spain and its Silent Past*. New York: Bloomsbury USA, 2008.

Williams, Mark. *The Story of Spain: The Dramatic History of One of Europe's Most Fascinating Countries*. Málaga: Santana Books, 2000.

Zollo, Mike with Phil Turk. *Spanish Language, Life, and Culture*. London: Teach Yourself Books, 2000.

Spanish. A Complete Course. New York: Living Language, 2005.

Fodor's Spanish for Travelers. New York: Living Language, 2005.

PICTURE CREDITS

INDEX